Contents

Preface

P olitics can be a dirty word.

For many, the word itself produces disgust. But "politics" can mean a myriad of things. I will explain what I mean by politics in the introduction, but for now let me set expectations and detail what this book is *not*.

What This Book Is Not

This book is not an argument for one party over another. I don't have a secret agenda to make you conservative or progressive, right or left. My goal is not to get you to vote one way or another in the future. Neither you nor I know what the future holds.

This book is also not a manual for policies. I won't go into different issues and give categories for how to think about them. Ethical triage needs to be done at some point, but there are other books for that.

And related to these two things, this book is not simply an argument for a third way. Good resides in third-wayism, but sometimes

it amounts to simply being a criticizer rather than a creator, a pro-
testor rather than a planner.

Instead, this book offers a paradigm, a framework from which
to think. It is a book aimed at *political discipleship*. One of the problems with our politics is that we often start with the issues and don't
have a solid foundation from which to build.

I hope this book can be part of a structural framework. I hope
it will allow for complexity, paradox, and different conclusions
based on various circumstances and social locations. I hope one
will leave recognizing Christianity is quite political, but maybe not
in the way you think.

Writing a book about politics provides abundant opportunities
to offend. I'm exploring a paradox, and certain chapters are meant
to be read together. If you feel yourself saying, "Yes, but," please
read the next chapter before you jump to judgment.

One other comment is necessary. While I aimed to write this
book for all Christians thinking about politics, I couldn't escape
being a white Protestant Westerner situated within American politics. Though I hope my principles can be applied in various contexts, I aim more directly at what it means to exist as a Christian in
the political landscape of the United States.

Political Gospel

The barber was just down Hawthorne Boulevard, a few blocks from the school where I taught.

The school was a strange place to work. We were an evangelical seminary sitting on one of Portland, Oregon's most notorious streets. On these sidewalks individualism reigns—strange haircuts and strange getups as far as the eye can see.

Google "The Unipiper" and you'll see what I mean.

I enjoyed being on Hawthorne Boulevard. It's a taste of where culture is going. It's all about authenticity, whether in food or personal expression. On Hawthorne, you find a people group who need the gospel, no more or less than anyone else.

But that day, I needed to get my hipster fade. No one gives a good hipster fade like a Portland barber. My barber and I got into the normal type of conversation when you get a haircut. She asked me what I did.

"I teach theology," I told her.

She looked at me quizzically and asked, "Why?"

Portlanders don't regularly meet theology professors. It was like I was from Mars, or the days when people watched *Home Improvement* with Tim Allen.

I knew there were two traps to avoid in answering her question (as it was a gospel opportunity).

First, I had to steer away from partisan politics.

Most people in Portland know about evangelicals from MSNBC. Poll Portlanders and they won't say evangelicals are known for their love of Jesus and their neighbor. They think all evangelicals are Republicans, which in Portland (whether for the right or wrong reasons) immediately hinders gospel conversations. I had to tread carefully.

But there was another pitfall I wanted to avoid. I didn't want to communicate my beliefs were merely a personal conviction. They are a personal conviction, but they are much more than that.

I was tired of people saying, "Well that sounds nice *for you*. I'm glad that works *for you*." Portlanders are all about letting you do what you want to do. They are all about *your* truth, defined by the sovereign "I."

I had the opportunity to share the gospel, but I wanted to avoid these two ditches. What was I to say?

The typical evangelical answer comes in this sort of form: *God loves you and wants to have a relationship with you. But you have pushed yourself away from God and now he wants you to come back. You can only come back through Jesus.*

Now, there is a lot of good in this answer, but there are two problems. First, to say God loves you confuses people, because they are not sure they want to love God. They are not convinced he is good. Second, we need to think bigger. "God loves you," while true, is not really the story of the Bible. It's too narrow. The Bible paints a grander vision.

So rather than giving an immediate answer, I said, "Well, because I'm interested in the big questions of life, like: *Why are we here? What are we to do? What went wrong? Where are we going?*"

As she was cleaning her clipper she asked, "Well, what did you find out?"

Great opportunity, right?

It was at this point that I had a few minutes to summarize the message of Jesus. How was I to do this? What sort of answer was I to give? What sort of answer would you give?

Political Gospel

My argument in this book is that *Christianity is political.* Though it might sound crazy in our supercharged political climate, I don't think the average Christian is nearly political enough.

It has become a truism to state that Jesus didn't come with a political message. As the common trope goes, though Israel expected a warrior-king to come riding on a white horse to over-throw Rome, he came with a spiritual message about their hearts. Jesus simply wants a relationship with you.

The problem is, this is a half-truth.

Jesus made a political announcement. He declared himself to be King. We have one ruler to whom we are loyal.

Kanye West popularized this political message with his album *Jesus Is King*. However, many still think "Jesus is King" means, "He is Lord of my life." We forget Jesus is more than that; he is the King *of kings*.

Jesus was not "conservative" or "progressive," but we must not miss the politics of Jesus. The whole biblical story line can be put under the banner of politics.

- God put humans here to rule the earth.
- Sin is insurrection.
- Redemption is the offer of amnesty and citizenship in a new kingdom.
- Restoration is the empire come.

Rule out politics, and you throttle the proclamation of God's saving power. Almost all the vocabulary of salvation (justification, peace, faithfulness, and kingdom of God) has a political dimension. The substance of Christian hope at its foundation is political. Thus, Jesus was not merely urging a revolution in personal values. He was not aloof to political concerns; it was the very purpose of his coming.

I hope to show you that the spheres of religion and politics are not only partially overlapping, but completely and wholly overlapping. Yet, maybe not in the way you think.

Politics Defined

When you hear me arguing for a more "political" understanding of the gospel message, you might mistakenly assume a few things.

First, you might think I'm speaking about a partisanship. Many equate being *political* with being *partisan*, but politics is larger than partisanship. I'm not arguing we should do more wheeling and dealing along party lines, or that pastors should endorse candidates. I'm not arguing Jesus can be smuggled into one of our political parties or that preachers should be more like politicians. That is not what I mean by "political."

Second, you might think I'm arguing for the merging of church and state. While instituting Christian law into our political processes is a complex topic, we need to recognize the authority of the church and the authority of governing officials are distinct. We must not imitate imperialist forms of religion: the Spanish Inquisition, Charlemagne, the cross-carrying conquistadors, the Nazi co-option of Christianity— these are all corruptions of Christianity's political vision. We have seen through history that using political power to implement God's law ends in disaster.

> **Using political power to implement God's law ends in disaster.**

If I don't mean these things, then what do I mean?

My subject is politics in the historical sense of the word. I mean politics in terms of public life, the ordering of society, enacting justice, and the arranging of common goods.

"Political" simply means *the activities associated with the organization and governance of people.* It has to do with rulership and who has the right to order our lives. It is what happens in the public domain. To paraphrase Augustine, politics is people bound together by common loves.[1]

Politics comes from the Greek word *polis* which means city, or *politikia* meaning the affairs of the cities. In some ways, "a political

---

[1] Augustine, *City of God,* in *Nicene and Post-Nicene Fathers,* Series 1.

gospel" simply means a public reality, and the governance of that public activity, as opposed to a private or individualistic one.

God is sovereign over the whole world, not merely the inner reaches of the human heart. His project includes the ordering of society, of public life, the establishment of a coming city, and even its present manifestation in the church.

But I'm also not merely suggesting Christianity has political *implications*. Christianity is itself a politic.

It is an all-encompassing vision of the world and human life. This all-encompassing vision is meant to be enacted in the church, showcased to our neighbors, and spread to the world.

Politics answers the questions: *How do we live together? How do we deal with money? How do we treat our enemies? What is authority? How should we love? Whom should we love? What does it mean to be human? How do we form communities? What is justice? Who is in charge? And how do we disagree?*

> **Christian politics concerns how we integrate our confession that Jesus is Lord with our call to love our neighbors.**

Politics is simply how we partner together for the flourishing of humanity and the world. We must open the horizon of politics past partisanship and allow God to have his say again.

Christian politics concerns how we integrate our confession that Jesus is Lord with our call to love our neighbors.

Many people wonder if Jerusalem has anything to do with Athens, but it should also be asked whether Bethlehem has anything to say about Rome? The answer is actually quite easy.

King Herod, the puppet of Rome, didn't kill the baby boys in Bethlehem because a spiritual guru was born. He killed them because a new Ruler had arrived, and he knew his days were numbered.

That is why Jesus was crucified on a Roman cross. Why Peter was crucified by Nero upside-down. Why Paul was beheaded by the same Caesar. Their messages were the tremors of a new regime.

Putting Politics in Its Place

But why is this important now? Aren't we trying to get people to be less political in the church, not more? Recovering the true political nature of our message is vital because it puts politics in its proper place.

By putting politics in its place I mean two things. First, the church in many places has become *partisan*. Political loyalties need to be demoted. In America, some gatherings become a seat for the Donkey or Elephant to gain loyalists. We swallow whole the red or blue pill. Into the matrix we go.

Most political discipleship comes from talking heads on cable news, not from reflections on the implications of our faith for public life. I have stopped counting the number of stories I have heard of pastors telling me they have been fired, or their congregants have left, because their message was getting too political or was not political enough.

No matter what you think about what happened from 2016 to 2021 in America, the evidence suggests churches have failed to disciple people in the realm of political engagement. Many are leaving churches over politics before they will leave their politics for a church.[2]

The fire-hydrant of partisan news is winning hearts. A thirty-minute sermon floats like a speck on the ocean surface of cable news. We are what we eat. While most of us theoretically know the gospel transcends political partisanship and division, it is another thing to put that into practice.

Second, we need to put politics in its place in a positive sense. Some churches and Christians, in reaction to this partisanship, have *privatized* their faith. Not much is said about how the gospel should shape our public habits or stances. Without knowing it, we begin to engrave a distinction between personal and political ethics. However, this distinction is hard to maintain.

> The fire-hydrant of partisan news is winning hearts. A thirty-minute sermon floats like a speck on the ocean surface of cable news.

Do Jesus's words "Blessed are the peacemakers" in Matthew 5:9 apply to individuals or communities? The correct answer is, *yes*.

Too often the church has become politically quietistic or innocuous. But only the privileged have this opportunity. The black slave families in the American South knew politics matter. Women in the 1920s knew. Cuban immigrants who sought to escape Castro knew. Hebrew slaves in Egypt knew. Those who experienced

---

[2] I saw Derwin Gray say this on Twitter.

Hurricane Katrina knew. And Jesus knew that politics matter as he was nailed onto a Roman cross.[3]

In sum, putting politics in its proper place means recovering the political nature of our message. And we need to recover our political gospel because *our political discipleship has become malformed.* While Christians are quick to speak, write, and reflect on marriage, vocation, and spiritual practices, fewer attempt to address how Christianity is itself a politic.

As Christians we desire to bring every part of our lives in conformity with Christ. Every corner, every back alley, every uncharted spot in our life must be touched by the hand of Jesus. This includes our political lives.

We have more work to do in political discipleship.

So to clear the ground we have to go back to the New Testament. In Jesus's time, the division we have constructed between religion and politics was not a given. Furthermore, it was not a given throughout most of history. The question of whether Jesus was a religious or political figure would have made little sense to a first-century individual.

The problem can be summarized in this way: Christianity is political, but it has been "partisanized." Christianity is public, but it has been privatized.

---

[3] I paraphrase some of this language from Lee Camp, *Scandalous Witness: A Little Political Manifesto for Christians* (Grand Rapids: Eerdmans, 2020), 6.

Christians and Politics

Option 1 ───────── Faithfulness ───────── Option 2

Private ───────── Political ───────── Partisan

The Paradox

My focus in this book will be on one tension, or paradox, that we find difficult. To claim Jesus's message is political is one thing. However, to say *in what way* it is political is another thing. Imagine with me a scenario.[4]

In the distant future a spaceship parks over New York City. A group of humanoids deboard claiming they are from a distant planet. They are a strange group. Though they look like humans in that they walk upright on two legs, they have small heads, no hair, and a blueish tint. They tell earth-humans that they represent a new era. They are just a delegation; there are thousands of ships on the way. They claim this new era will change how we live for the good.

Obviously, earth-humans would be nervous about what this means. It sounds like these humanoids want to colonize earth. But the humanoids explain they have a communication tool that will make our lives better. Justice will reign. Everything will be fair. No one will be left out. In fact, they go further than this. They invite

---

[4] A similar example appears in Jonathan Leeman's book, *How the Nations Rage* (Nashville: Nelson Books, 2018), 114. I have changed the details and illustration to some extent.

people to view glimpses of this tool weekly, where they talk about how to live like the future is already present.

These humanoids go to great lengths to connect with earth-humans. They begin dressing like them, eating like them—in some respect, acting like them.

Though assumptions spread about insurrection, when asked pointedly on CNN, the humanoids affirm they support the current governing authorities and will submit to them. When asked whether they will continue to support the governing authorities when the rest of their fleet arrives with the new technology, they say the governing authorities will no longer be necessary. Their tool will accomplish what the government has been trying to do all these years. In the meantime, they are happy to support them, as long as they preserve society until their gift arrives.

How would you feel about such a group?

I'm sure you would have some mixed feelings. In one sense they sound like a threat to society. In another sense, it sounds like they genuinely want to do good. They can support what is happening now, but they also say a new era is arriving. They are representatives of it, and they don't seem to be hiding any ill will.

I will argue a very similar tension exists in the Scriptures.

- Christians are, in a sense, alien delegates to the world from a different kingdom.
- Churches are colonies of the kingdom that give the world a foretaste of what life will be like when Christ returns.

- Jesus called the Roman rulers tyrants and foxes, but also said to submit to them and pay taxes to Caesar.

- Both Jesus and Paul were brought before the power of the state and condemned. However, they were also both innocent of sedition.

- Romans 13 commands us to submit to governing authorities, but Revelation 13 also says the governing authorities power stems from Satan.

The paradox shows Christians both are a political threat and are not a political threat. Early Christians sought not to provoke political strife, but their very presence did so at times. As Kavin Rowe puts it, Christianity says: "new culture, yes—coup, no."[5] It is this tension we need to recover for our modern political engagement.

The gospel message is a world-forming, public, and political reality. Jesus calls people to a new way of life, a new society, a new community. In this way, Jesus and Paul contested the current order of society.

Jesus doesn't allow you to lock him in your political box.

Yet at the same time, Jesus is after no earthly throne. Rome was not the main problem. Jesus and

[5] Rowe repeats this line throughout his book. C. Kavin Rowe, *World Upside Down: Reading Acts in the Graeco-Roman Age* (Oxford University Press, 2010), 5.

Paul were not guilty of revolution, and Christians were not even forbidden from serving the state.

How can both of these things be true? How can Christians offer a radically subversive political message and be submissive to the ruling authorities?

Some tend to emphasize being submissive to the government, while others tend to emphasize Jesus's subversive message. Some speak of Jesus as "meek and mild" while others show Jesus was a "political revolutionary." Some focus more on Jesus's word to love your enemies, while others capitalize on Jesus's action in the temple. The reality is, both exist simultaneously.

Jesus doesn't allow you to lock him in your political box.

Pause and Reflect

You might want to pause at this point and think about your church tradition. At the risk of oversimplification, because of social privileges, majority white churches in the United States have tended to emphasize submitting to government authorities while majority black churches have been more thoughtful about biblical subversion. Or, to give another example, house churches in communist countries must think carefully about subversion, while party-sanctioned churches must think carefully about submission.

The problem is when one of these becomes a totalizing view of Christianity. Subversion and submission are both true. They somehow fit together. It's a paradox.

We need to learn from one another.

The aim of this book is to explore the paradox. Eugene Peterson puts the point well: "The gospel of Jesus Christ is more political than anyone imagines, but in a way that no one guesses."[6]

The Plan of This Book

While there are many good books on politics, this one differs in several ways. Rather than focusing on *issues* (immigration, climate change, abortion, religious freedom), I want to provide a *framework* for thinking through political discipleship and our public witness.

We get this framework from the Bible, even though no verse or section comprises our entire political theology. We have some assembly to do.

We must remember that Jesus and early Christians also lived under a political system. So, we not only have some theological assembly to do; we have some historical and cultural work to do as well.[7] We will do this by comparing the Christian message to that of Rome and its emperors.

This book doesn't contain everything one could say about political theology. My aim is narrower. I am not only arguing Christianity is political, but also focusing on two actions based on

---

[6] Eugene H. Peterson, *Reversed Thunder: The Revelation of John and the Praying Imagination* (San Francisco: HarperOne, 1991), 117.

[7] Many political theory and theology books have surprisingly little to say about how Christians interacted with the Roman Empire. This might be because we are prone to focus on Jewish backgrounds rather than Roman backgrounds, but we have much to learn from early postures toward governing authorities. A chasm separates historical studies and political theology (at least in my field). It's time to build a bridge across this abyss. We should look at how Jesus and early Christians responded to the Roman Empire and then draw principles from their interaction for our own political formation and public witness.

one major truth. The truth is this: *human governments are subordinate to God's rule.* God is in charge and humans must align themselves with his purposes. His authority over our lives is of a different order than the authority of governing officials.

Though this sounds simple, it has massive implications.

Because God is our authority, *we are to subvert and submit to governing authorities.* While we might think these are contradictory responses, they both stem from the same conviction.

To trace the paradox of subversion and submission, I have divided this book into three sections. First, we will look at our *political past,* focusing on Jesus's politically subversive message but submissive presence. Then we will examine our *political present* and see how the church turned the world upside down but was also declared innocent. Finally, we will look toward our *political future* and see how the kingdom of God conquers all other kingdoms but does so by God's citizens being martyrs.

The structure of the book can be viewed through three words that indicate the political nature of our faith. The first section concerns the "gospel," the second the "church," and the final section Jesus's "return." All of these are political terms.

Political Structure		
Political Past	Gospel	Jesus's announcement of victory
Political Present	Church	A political assembly
Political Future	Return	The return of a ruler

In all of these we will refer to Christianity under the banner of "The Way," following the book of Acts, displaying the paradox and tension of Christian political discipleship.

- Jesus proclaimed the *way of the kingdom* but enacted it as the *way of the dove*.
- Paul proclaimed the *way of subversion* but did so in the *way of submission*.
- Jesus's return will be the *way of the lion* but embodied in the *way of a slain lamb*.

The Gospel and Portland: Reprise

So how did I answer my barber in Portland when she asked me the basic message of Christianity? How was I to avoid giving an answer she could shrug at and say, "Nice for you," but also one where she wouldn't think I was trying to persuade her to join a political party?

My answer was probably not very good, but what I tried to do was set up the Bible's grand kingdom and King narrative. I told her a story about politics.

I said, "God is in the process of making a beautiful garden-city where, because of the new King's governance and wisdom, there will be no more pain, sadness, division, violence, hurt, and hate.

"That was always the plan. God has always intended humans to rule earth with him. But we have all turned and attempted to create our own kingdoms. We created Babylons, evil cities where we redefine evil and good and fight one another. These are opposed to God's good design.

"So God has graciously provided our true and undeserved Monarch, who died on the cross and is in the process of making a new society. God requires us to pledge loyalty to his Son and start living the kingdom life now amid dark and broken kingdoms."

"Interesting," she said, as she paused and looked at me for a moment. Then she finished cutting my hair.

Perhaps she found it interesting because I presented it as a public reality instead of a partisan reality. A political reality and not only a personal relationship.

The gospel is political.

That means your Christianity is not private.

That means your Christianity is public.

That means your Christianity is not, as the Dude in *The Big Lebowski* said, "Just, like, your opinion, man."

PART 1

POLITICAL PAST

CHAPTER 1

The Way of the Kingdom

Jesus's Subversive Revolution

In August 2012, I received a phone call I'll never forget.

My dad called and said Mom had been in a terrible bicycle accident. We needed to go the hospital ASAP. She hit her head so hard against the pavement that they didn't know if she would live.

When we saw her in the hospital the swelling had progressed so much that we barely recognized her. After a four-hour surgery, the doctors were able to relieve the pressure from the swelling, and she started to recover.

Yet all was not well. When she became cognizant, I remember bringing my two daughters up to see her. When I asked if she remembered their names, she shook her head no. You could tell in her eyes she knew she should remember. She wanted to badly, but she couldn't.

Part of her rehab included a lot of mental exercises. The doctor said her brain was like a filing cabinet. When she hit her head, the cabinet turned over, and all its contents were strewn out on the floor. Her recovery would include refiling things. I remember sitting by her while the doctor held up a spoon and asked what it was called. She shook her head indicating she couldn't remember.

Even a few years later, when she had largely recovered, she would sometimes look at something like an ambulance and ask, "What do you call that again?"

Like my mom, we are all in the process of filing and refiling things in our brains.

Language works by association. Words run certain "scripts" in our minds. We file things in certain folders to make sense of the world. For example, when you see these words you file them in the same folder.

Doctor / Hospital / Stretcher

In this case, the script these words run for me center on my mom's accident. For you, the script might be general ideas like "health care" or "medical field."

In the same way, we file Christian words in certain folders. Take the following words, for example:

Gospel / Kingdom / Believe

We might put all of these into a larger folder called "religion" or "personal belief." But this raises certain questions: Would the first Christians have put these words there? How would they have categorized them? What scripts ran in their minds when they heard these terms? I want to suggest that the primary script that would have run in their mind was "politics."

Political Words

When Jesus stepped onto the scene, his first words were fully political: "The time is fulfilled, and the kingdom of God is at hand; repent and believe in the gospel" (Mark 1:15 ESV). Gospel. Kingdom. Believe. All of these are politically loaded terms and need to be filed correctly.

Gospel

It would be an understatement to say the term *gospel* is an important term in the Scriptures. Not only is it central in Scripture, but churches have adopted the term as their most beloved adjective. You have gospel churches, gospel-centered ministries, gospel-centered websites, sermons, discipleship, parenting, community, counseling, parents, family, youth ministry, teaching, marriage, kids' ministry, and hospitality.

If all the gospel-centered titles were collected, I suppose not even the world itself could contain the books that have been written. But confusion still exists about what this term actually means. What did *gospel* mean in Jesus's day? Where did it come from? How was it used? A survey of its use both in the Bible and outside the Bible reveals that "gospel" was a term that communicated *political victory*.

In literature outside of the Bible, "to gospelize" is the activity of a messenger with a beneficial report. The messenger was sent from the field of battle by ship, horse, or on foot to proclaim victory. Usually this was associated with the defeat of an army, or the death or capture of an enemy.

Also included in this was the news of a ruler's birth, coming of age, or enthronement. A calendar inscription speaks of the birth of the emperor Augustus as "the beginning of good news" for the world.

> "[Augustus] . . . has made war to cease and . . . put
> everything in peaceful order; and . . . the birthday
> of our god [emperor] signaled the beginning of
> 'the gospel' for the world because of him."[1]

Another decree says the appearance of Caesar exceeded the hopes of all those who anticipated *gospel*.[2] An inscription speaks of the "gospel of Rome's victory." The Roman general Pompey was given the message of the death of his adversary under the umbrella of gospel.[3]

In summary, "gospel" was connected to emperors, politics, and military victory.

The Bible confirms the political meaning of *gospel*. Jesus was a Jew, so he used terms in line with not only the culture of the time but of the Old Testament. In the Old Testament, *gospel* also means political victory.

In 1 Samuel 31:9 the enemies of Israel, the Philistines, cut off King Saul's head. They sent the news of this victory (the gospel) to all the Philistines. The gospel was an announcement of victory, in this case the beheading of the opposing king.

---

[1] Adolf Deissmann and Lionel Richard Mortimer Strachan, *Light from the Ancient East: The New Testament Illustrated by Recently Discovered Texts of the Greco-Roman World* (London: Hodder & Stoughton, 1910), 371.

[2] Bruce Winter, *Divine Honours for the Ceasars: The First Christian's Responses* (Grand Rapids: Eerdmans, 2015), 37.

[3] Plutarch, *Pompeius* 66.3.

In 2 Kings 6–7, Elisha finds himself surrounded by the king of Aram who lays siege to Samaria. They block all of Samaria's resources, and a severe famine occurs. It gets so bad the Samaritans begin eating their children.

Elisha promises God will save them, and the next day four messengers find the Arameans' camp abandoned. The Arameans left all their tents, horses, and donkeys. The four messengers say, "Today is a day of [*gospel*]. . . . So let's go tell the king's household" (2 Kings 7:9). Gospel is the announcement of political victory.

The prophet Isaiah proclaims the "gospel" of God coming to rescue his people from exile (Isa. 52:7). The Spirit of Yahweh is upon the messenger to bring "gospel," which is further defined as "bind[ing] up the brokenhearted, proclaim[ing] liberty to the captives, . . . the opening of the prison to those who are bound" (Isa. 61:1 ESV).

Jesus himself picks up this language from Isaiah 61 as the manifesto for his ministry in Nazareth (Luke 4:16–19). To give liberty to the captive, bind up the brokenhearted, and to open the prison for people cannot be measured merely by spiritual realities.

This background on the term *gospel* may help rearrange your filing cabinet. The cultural script that should come to your mind for "gospel" is the birth of a king or the conquest of an emperor. After his victory, an emissary would ride into town and announce the "gospel" of this ruler's victory. The good news means a new order had arrived. Therefore, to proclaim a "gospel" in Jesus's day was an implicit challenge to the established ruler.[4]

---

[4] As N. T. Wright observes: "To come to Rome with the gospel of Jesus, to announce someone else's accession to the world's throne, therefore, was to put on a red coat and walk into a field with a potentially angry bull." N. T. Wright,

Kingdom

Imagine a young Elon Musk waltzing into the Ford Motor Company talking about a new kingdom for the car industry. He proclaims the future of automobiles is electric. He wouldn't even have to say anything directly negative about Ford; his insinuations would be apparent.

Ford's owners might ignore him as a crazy man, or they might be more concerned about his message. Either way, they would not be too keen on another Musk visit. They would likely show him the door—or worse.

Any challenge to the status quo has consequences. Jesus came announcing a new kingdom, and he suffered the penalties. Jesus did not proclaim a mere "gospel," but spoke of the gospel "of" or "concerning" *the kingdom*.

Many evangelicals are comfortable with the language of gospel, but we trip over the language of kingdom. It sounds too political, too authoritarian. Or maybe we associate it with the theologically liberal social gospel of the 1900s, so, we separate kingdom and gospel to avoid confusion.

However, according to Jesus, you can't understand the gospel without understanding the kingdom. The two are intimately related. It would be like trying to understand Martin Luther King Jr.'s message without the civil rights movement, or Alexander Hamilton's writings without the Revolutionary War.

"Romans," in *The New Interpreters Bible*, vol. 10 (Nashville: Abingdon Press, 2002), 423.

If Jesus's message is good news, the content of this good news is the kingdom. The tight relationship between the gospel and the kingdom can be seen in Jesus's own words.

- "The time is fulfilled, and the *kingdom of God* has come near. Repent and believe the *good news!*" (Mark 1:15, emphasis added).
- "Now Jesus began to go all over Galilee, teaching in their synagogues, preaching the *good news of the kingdom*, and healing every disease and sickness among the people" (Matt. 4:23, emphasis added).

The kingdom Jesus announced is a new society, a new social and political order. We could almost translate kingdom as empire, dynasty, or monarchy. Try that out next time you talk about Jesus's message. You'll likely get some strange looks.

Monarchy is God's sacred mission on the earth. Without a central understanding of kingship and kingdom as the backdrop to everything in the Bible, not much of it will make sense.

If Jesus's message is good news, the content of this good news is the kingdom.

Many Christmas cards I receive each year have texts like Isaiah 9:6 on the back. I always wonder if the smiling faces understand the radical political statement they are making with this greeting.

> For a child will be born for us,
> a son will be given to us,

and the government will be on his shoulders.
He will be named
Wonderful Counselor, Mighty God,
Eternal Father, Prince of Peace.

These are political claims. When Jesus pronounced the coming of the kingdom of God, he indicated God's rule as being *made visible* on the earth through his person. The problem should be obvious: other kingdoms already exist. They're inevitably going to bump into one another.

In this way, Jesus's message is radically subversive. That's why Herod sought to kill him when he was born. That's why the Sadducees and Pharisees, who were not only religious but also political leaders, sought to end his life. That's why Satan was opposed to his coming.

We cannot privatize and depoliticize Jesus's message and say he was establishing the rule of God in people's hearts or simply winning souls. This is eons away from what Jesus announced. Jesus's message brought him to a Roman cross. Above his head hung the charge: "the King of the Jews."

Believe

In Mark 1:15, Jesus says in order to enter this new *polis* (city), people need to believe. But what does it mean to believe?

The common way of thinking about belief/faith in English is a subjective and inward trust. When you type "faith" into Google, one of the first definitions that arises is "strong belief in God or in the doctrines of a religion, based on a spiritual apprehension rather than proof."[5]

For many, faith is the opposite of evidence-based truth. It is an irrational leap in the dark that believes God's invisible realities even though we can't see them. Faith is like Harrison Ford in *Indiana Jones and the Last Crusade* when he stands at the edge of a long dark chasm and takes a step of faith, landing on an invisible bridge. In the same way, we must have faith because we can't see or touch Jesus.

But is this what Jesus meant when he said to believe the gospel?

The term *faith* didn't always occur in political contexts. However, when it is used in close relationship to gospel and kingdom, it should be interpreted in a political frame.

The Christian tradition has always recognized that faith includes both an internal and external reality. To get at the external sense, "loyalty" and "allegiance" can be good translations.

Once again, it is helpful to step outside the Bible to see the script associated with faith in Roman cultures. *Pistis* (Greek for "faith") or *fides* (Latin word for "faith") is often used of the trustworthiness of commanders toward their men, and the devotion of both to their state, king, or emperor.

The title *pia fidelis* (Latin for "loving, faithful") was awarded by the emperor to certain men or legions who had proved to be devoted and loyal. Claudius gave the title *pia fidelis* to the Seventh and Ninth Legions for their loyalty during a revolt.

During the Roman civil wars of 48 BC, a standard-bearer was fatally wounded in a battle against Pompey. He died saying: "I have

---

[5] "Faith," definition #2, https://www.lexico.com/definition/faith.

defended this eagle living, for many years with great care, and now, dying, I restore it to Caesar with the same *fides*." Here he refers to his loyalty to Rome, which manifests itself in loyalty to Caesar.

In political contexts, "faith" is something others can see, something you direct toward rulers. Jesus announced the victory of his kingdom and told people they needed to believe in him. This means both inward and outward trust. Jesus announced the victory of his empire and told people they owed allegiance to him. The message Jesus was fully political.

> **Jesus announced the victory of his kingdom and told people they needed to believe in him.**

The Fox vs. the Lion

Some might still think Jesus avoided politics and though most of Jesus's verbal critique of Rome is implicit, one episode displays Jesus was not frightened to openly criticize governing authorities. In Luke 13:31–33 the Pharisees tell Jesus that Herod Antipas wants to kill Jesus. Readers should pause here to think through the implications.

This is the second Herod who wanted Jesus dead. Politicians were not fond of Jesus. The first Herod wanted to kill him while he was a still a baby. The second Herod beheaded John for critiquing the crown (Luke 3:19–20; 9:9; 13) and made no attempt to save Jesus when he went on trial (Luke 23:6–16). The Herods knew Jesus was a political figure; they were alarmed by the arrival of God's kingdom.

Jesus responds to Herod's death warrant with a piercing critique of Herod's reign. He says, "Go tell that fox, 'Look, I'm driving out demons and performing healings today and tomorrow, and on the third day I will complete my work'" (Luke 13:32).

No deference is paid to political authority. No compliment is given here. No softening the language for God's ordained ruler is conceded. To be called a fox is to be labeled a deceitful and cunning person. It is a contemptuous insult. Some later rabbis even note that a fox is an insignificant figure compared to a lion.

The lion of Judah roars and the Roman fox quakes (Gen. 49:9; Rev. 5:5). A new king was about to be installed on the third day right under Herod's nose.

The political witness of the church therefore includes more than "submitting to governing authorities." It includes subversive language against the corrupt and unethical ruling elite.

Jesus announced the victory of his empire and called people to loyalty. He even called the earthly ruler a fox. His message was political through and through. But as we will see, this new politic wouldn't start the way we might expect.

Political Actions

Not only Jesus's *words* but Jesus's *actions* need to be understood politically. Eventually, Jesus's actions led him to death row. While Jesus doesn't contest Rome directly, there are indirect signs that display Jesus as a criticizer, a modern-day opinion columnist of Roman rule.

The Exorcism of Legion

The longest exorcism story in the Gospels indicates a combative undertone toward Rome. In Mark 5:1–20 Jesus goes to the country of the Gerasenes, which is Gentile territory (5:1). There, Jesus steps off a boat and meets a man who emerges from the tombs with an unclean spirit. Death hangs in the air. This man lives socially ostracized among the dead.

When Jesus steps into this demon-infested territory, the possessed man falls before him, asking why the Son of God has come (5:6–7). Mark and his readers would have known that Roman emperors were also called "sons of god."

Jesus exorcizes the demons, an act of aggression and dominance. Notably, Jesus also asks the unclean spirit for his name. The focus on names is important. The unclean spirit has called Jesus "Son of God" while the name of the unclean spirit is revealed to be "Legion," for they are many (5:9).

A legion was the largest Roman military unit, consisting of five to six thousand violent soldiers. The exorcism *is* a story of personal liberation, but it is also a political parable. The true Son of God commands the Legion.

The Roman imagery continues. Legion begs Jesus not to send them out of the "country" (5:10 ESV; *chōras*). This term for "country" may evoke the image of a military unit occupying a particular place. Jesus then sees a great "herd" (*agelē*) of pigs feeding on the hillside. *Herd* is another term often used to describe military forces. He sends Legion into the pigs, and they "rush" down the steep bank into the sea (5:11–13). The verb "rushed" (*hormaō*) is a term sometimes employed for a military charge.[6] The pigs are significant too. A pig was the mascot or symbol of the tenth Roman legion stationed in Palestine. They carried a pig on their shields and banners.

A Political Exorcism in Mark 5	
Clue	**Roman Meaning**
Legion (5:9)	Primary definition of Roman imperial order. A legion was the largest Roman military unit, consisting of five to six thousand soldiers.
Out of the country (*chōras*; 5:10)	Evokes the image of military unit occupying a particular region
Herd (*agelē*; 5:11)	A word often used to describe military forces
Rushed (*hormaō*; 5:13)	A word commonly used to describe the charge of soldiers
Pigs	The tenth Roman legion stationed in Palestine carried the image of a boar on its shield and banners.

Though the supernatural element of this episode takes precedence, the baby doesn't need to be thrown out with the bathwater. The political relevance may not be the main point of this passage, but it is *a* point.

Mark alludes to the fact that Roman rule is sourced in supernatural forces—a reality that the apostle John would state more

---

[6] See Adam Winn, *Reading Mark's Christology Under Caesar: Jesus the Messiah and Roman Imperial Ideology* (Downers Grove, IL: IVP Academic, 2018), 81–85.

plainly in the book of Revelation. As Jesus binds Satan and plunders his house, he also plunders Rome's house, the Legion (Mark 3:27).

Rome has great military strength, but Jesus comes with greater power. Rome reeks of death, but Jesus comes with life. Rome binds, but Jesus sets free. Rome ostracizes, but Jesus welcomes. A new emperor has crossed the sea and come ashore. The forces of darkness recognize the true Son of God.

Jesus shows his dominance and subversion by taking one of Rome's mascots, the pig, and throwing it into the sea. Like Pharaoh's army, they oppressed God's people and were drowned. The true King has encountered a Legion and easily disarmed it. Jesus introduced a new kingdom to the possessed man.

Mark's subtle message is that Rome degrades, enslaves, and disrespects people; Jesus dignifies, frees, and esteems them. His coming was fully political.

Jesus's Trial

If I were to ask you why Jesus was crucified, what would you say? The correct answer is for our sins. But I mean why *historically* was he crucified? On what charges was Jesus nailed to a Roman cross? What accusations sent him to his death? Why was Jesus indicted?

Even when I clarify what question I'm asking, we might be quick to say that Jesus was crucified for religious claims. The Jewish leadership charged Jesus with blasphemy. When the high priest asks Jesus if he is the Messiah, Jesus affirms that he is the Son of Man

THE WAY OF THE KINGDOM   35

from Daniel 7. They will see him seated at the right hand of Power (Matt. 26:63–64).

The high priest tears his robes and cries out that Jesus has blasphemed; he deserves death (26:65–66). So in one sense, Jesus is charged with a religious claim. However, it is more complex than this for two reasons.

First, because religion and politics were not divided in the first century. When Jesus says he is the Son of Man who will be seated on a throne, this is both a political and religious claim. The book of Daniel is about the rise and fall of nations. Jesus claims to be the King of nations in his response. Jesus shot back with a religious and political assertion.

Second, we also tend to forget the question that Rome asks Jesus. Pilate asks Jesus, "Are you the king of the Jews?" In one sense, this is the same question the religious leaders posed. To be the Messiah is to be the King. But Pilate's question stems from his fear of rebellion. He wants to know if Jesus is a political rebel.

Jesus replies in an interesting way. In Matthew, Mark, and Luke, Jesus says, "You have said so." It is an enigmatic answer. He neither denies nor affirms. But in John, Jesus says, "You say that I am a king" (18:37). In the Roman Empire there was no king but Caesar (John 19:15). The Fourth Gospel shows we should interpret the other accounts in the affirmative. But it is a qualified affirmative. Jesus is not the type of king they expect. But he is a king.

Jesus was a king in disguise. Søren Kierkegaard tells the story of a prince who was eager to marry a maiden.[7] Near his palace was

---

[7] Søren Kierkegaard, "A King in Disguise," from *Daily Meditations and Prayers for the Christmas Advent Fast and Epiphany* by Presbytera Emily Harakas and Fr. Anthony Coniaris (Minneapolis: Light & Life Publishing Company, 2000).

a large city and one day he went through a poor section of the city and caught sight of a beautiful maiden.

He considered how he could marry her. He could order her to the palace, or he could ask her for her hand, or he could masquerade as a peasant and try to gain her interest. But none of these would work. Finally, he realized the only solution was to give up his kingly role and move into her neighborhood. There he would take up work and get acquainted with her life, concerns, interests, and even her language.

In due time he would make her acquaintance in a natural way, and she would hopefully come to love him as he loved her. Kierkegaard says this is what God did for us. He didn't order us to love him. He didn't appear to us as the King. He would win our love by becoming like us.

Unfortunately, people rejected Jesus both because he was a peasant and because he was the king. They were impressed neither with his humility nor his high claims. Therefore, they sent him to the cross saying that there was not room for another king. Ironically, in this action they crowned him as king.

When Jesus was crucified, the charge was put above his head. It reads, "This is Jesus of Nazareth, the King of the Jews." Jesus was crucified for political reasons.

Ascension to the Divine

Another act of aggression between Jesus and the emperors is his ascension (Luke 24:50–53; Acts 1:9–11). In the Roman world, ascension into heaven was accompanied with becoming a god. In Greek, this was called *apotheosis*, and in Latin *consecratio*.

When we read the Bible, the claims that Jesus is the Son of God, Lord, and Savior seem like religious claims. But in Jesus's context, these were also political titles. Roman emperors were deified and worshipped. Impressed into Roman coins was a bust of Caesar asserting he was the "son of God."

Rome customarily assigned divine status to its leaders. Citizens hailed Romulus, the founder of Rome, as a god, son of a god, king, and father of the city of Rome.[8] After Julius Caesar returned to Rome from a military victory, a statue was erected in the Capitol bearing the title "demigod."

Other titles like "Lord" and "Savior" ran a political script in Greco-Roman times, and to understand their significance, we need to refile them accordingly. An inscription about Julius Caesar says, "Gaius Julius Caesar . . . Chief Priest. . . . God made manifest and common Savior of Mankind."[9] The term *Lord* was used occasionally by emperors, most commonly by Nero. *Dominus*, which can be translated as Lord, became an official title for the emperor beginning with Diocletian (AD 284–305).

At a game held in his honor, Caesar Augustus confirmed the heavenly ascent of his stepfather. During the game, a comet appeared which, according to Augustus, was a sign that Julius Caesar had ascended into heaven. It was after this event that Augustus pressed the senate to affirm Julius Caesar's adopted status and therefore his status as an adopted son of god. This tradition continued as many emperors ascended to heaven and received the title of god.

---

[8] Livy, *The History of Rome*, Books 1–5, trans. Valerie M. Warrior (Indianapolis: Hackett Publications, 2006), 1:16.

[9] Corpus Inscriptionum Graecarum 2957 (48/47).

But Romans knew some of these claims were overplayed. The politician Seneca wrote a parody of the tyrannical rule of Claudius titled, *The Apocolocyntosis of the Divine Claudius*. *Apocolocyntosis* is a word play on *apotheosis*, meaning "Pumpkinification" or "Gourdification."

Seneca essentially mocks Claudius's ascension, pointing to his personal failings, most notably his arrogant cruelty and inarticulacy. This is evidence that the people recognized whether or not a ruler "deserved" the honor of *apotheosis*.

> Jesus occupies the highest throne. All the other kingdoms of the earth will be reduced to ashes and dust.

Under this cultural script, we can read Jesus's ascension as a subversive performance. By narrating Jesus's ascent into heaven, Luke asserts that Jesus is the true ascended Lord. Jesus is Lord. Caesar was not. Jesus occupies the highest throne. All the other kingdoms of the earth, as Daniel 7 said, will be reduced to ashes and dust.

Conclusion

Jesus asserted and enacted *the way of the kingdom*. He proclaimed, presented, and performed a new public, social, and political reality. When Pilate asked the Jews if he should crucify their king, they replied, "We have no king but Caesar" (John 19:15). No wonder Jesus was crucified on a Roman cross and mocked as a king. As C. S. Lewis once said:

Enemy-occupied territory—that is what this world is. Christianity is the story of how the rightful king has landed, you might say landed in disguise, and is calling us all to take part in a great campaign of sabotage.[10]

Jesus was not merely a teacher, a moralist, a sacrificial lamb, a counselor, a psychologist, or a spiritual guru. Jesus was the bearer of a new political regime.

However, these realities raise more questions than they answer. Some might think, because of the evidence presented in this chapter, that Jesus was an anarchist, revolutionary, or social reformer, and that we should act similarly. Others might be tempted to apply Jesus's subversiveness to everything they don't currently like about their governmental system. We say things like, "Jesus would be subversive about _____! I know it!"

When we do this, we create a political Jesus in our image. How many of our manufactured Jesuses have all the same policy views as we do?

This is where we have to remember what we said at the beginning of this book—Christian political discipleship is a paradox. Jesus's subversive political message must be clearly defined and paired with other texts. We'll turn to some of those other texts now, as we see how Jesus models the way of the dove.

---

[10] C. S. Lewis, *Mere Christianity* (New York: Harper Collins, 2001), 45–46.

CHAPTER 2

The Way of the Dove

Jesus's Surprising Submission

The Apostles' Creed, one of our earliest summaries of the Christian faith, states, "Jesus suffered under Pontius Pilate."

It is an odd item to include in a confessional statement. Most of the Creed speaks to what many would call theological realities: Jesus's nature, his death, burial, resurrection, and ascension.

However, the early church also recognized the political reality of Jesus's life. The line about Pilate reminds us Jesus was a political figure. He lived his life under the political power of the Roman army and in the shadow of Caesar's statue. He traveled on Roman roads, traded with Roman coins, and walked by Roman temples.

Jesus lived in the midst of the Roman Empire, was brought before them, and was crucified as a dissident to the state. Crucifixion was the punishment for agitators.[1] He hung on the cross as a political rebel.

The early creed recognized the importance of Jesus's political context. He did not come as a psychologist, entrepreneur, or even a mere religious leader. He came as a king. But there was another king on the throne—Caesar, the so-called "son of god." The two would inevitably clash.

The last chapter examined this clash, as we looked at Jesus's subversive political message and actions. This might lead some to think Jesus was an insurrectionist. But Jesus was anything but mutinous.

The Gospels link Jesus's subversiveness with his submissiveness. Paradoxically, the two come together. Jesus's claims were political, but they were political in a way people could hardly imagine.

The Gospels link Jesus's subversiveness with his submissiveness.

God's kingdom does not come by the sword, but through the flight of the dove. It would not come when or as Rome expected. Rome didn't have the framework to understand this revolution.

The Baptism: A Dove Conquers the Eagle

In America and England, birds are symbols of authority and power. Look at the back of the American quarter. There, an

---

[1] For details on crucifixion as punishment in the Roman Empire, see Martin Hengel, *Crucifixion,* trans. John Bowden (Philadelphia: Fortress Press, 1977), 33–63.

eagle stands with its wings spread proudly. The eagle's presence is also noticeable in England's royal consecration. The Dean of Westminster pours consecrated oil from an eagle-shaped vessel into a spoon, which the Archbishop of Canterbury uses to anoint the sovereign. But why eagles?

Both of these traditions hail from earlier times. The Romans practiced augury (where we get the term *inauguration*). Augury refers to what will happen in the future, usually in observation of the birds. Birds were understood as signs sent by the gods as an indication of their will. They were messengers from heaven to the earth. Through birds, the god Jupiter (Zeus) communicated to Rome.

The flight of the birds was the surest of all omens, and the eagle was the strongest and most reliable of all augural signs. Eagles symbolized power and authority, establishing a candidate's claim to the throne. Because the eagle had a distinctive relationship with Jupiter, it became the emblem of the Roman Empire.

Roman tradition tells the story of Romulus, who founded the city in obedience to the auspices. His brother Remus was the first to receive an augury, the flight of six vultures. However, Romulus saw twice the number of birds. At this sign Romulus was declared king.

This continued in the traditions of the Roman emperors. Octavian was named *Augustus* because of the augural rites. Tiberius (AD 14–36), Augustus's adopted son, was also elected because omens preceded his succession. Years before becoming an emperor, Tiberius returned home, and an eagle appeared on the roof of his house. Before Claudius (41–54) became emperor, when he entered the Forum, an eagle came and landed on his shoulder. An augural omen in the last year of Nero's life signaled the end of his dynasty. Vespasian, the first in the Flavian Dynasty, had an augural confirmation.

In light of this practice, the Spirit descending like a dove on Jesus at his baptism becomes a more potent symbol. The descent of the dove not only reveals Christ's royal anointing; it also shows his royal crowning was antithetical to Rome's domineering power; a different kingdom had arrived. Rather than an eagle, a dove descends on Jesus. Eagles are symbols for war and strength. Doves symbolize peace, purity, serenity, and gentleness.

The dove confirms the political nature of Jesus's message and ministry, yet it also indicates Jesus's political program was radically different from Rome's. He was establishing a different kind of kingdom.

Jesus would not conquer by the sword, but by sacrifice.

Though his message challenges the rulers, he would not take up arms against them. Though his message demands rulers to do good, he would submit to them.

A baptismal dove conquers the imperial eagle. The dove shows Jesus's kingdom was one of peace. Jesus was not after Caesar's throne. He was constructing a different kind of kingdom, so much so that when Caesar saw it, he wouldn't even recognize Jesus as a king of a kingdom. Jesus proclaimed the gospel of the kingdom, but it came by the flight of a dove.

Jesus's Ethical Teaching

At night, when I put the kids to bed, I will sing them a song. It's a way to calm them down and give them rituals to mark their days. It also ends their days with the truth of God's beauty in their ears. Many times, they will ask for new songs, and I won't know what to sing, so I'll retrieve songs from my childhood. One night I remembered an old song I learned in Sunday school: "I'm in the Lord's Army." The words go like this:

> I may never march in the infantry
> Ride in the cavalry
> Shoot the artillery
> I may never zoom o'er the enemy
> But I'm in the Lord's army.

Though simple, this song has pretty good political theology. If Jesus were starting a typical revolution, he would gather an army and train them for war. If Jesus were an anarchist, zealot, or insurrectionist, we would expect to hear exhortations to subvert the political system. Perhaps he would recruit soldiers to change social structures by force.

However, Jesus's message for his followers instructed them on nonretaliation, enemy love, and peace. Jesus preached a politic of persuasion, a seminar of servanthood, not instruction on insurrection.[2] In Jesus's sermons, we find the ethics of a dove.

Jesus doesn't preach, "Blessed are troublemakers, the revolutionaries, and the mutineers." He says, "Blessed are the poor in spirit, the mourners, merciful, peacemakers, and those who are persecuted" (see Matt. 5:3–12). His kingdom is for the weak, those

---

[2] I used this phrase "politic of persuasion" from Stanley Hauerwas, "Church Matters," in *Christian Political Witness* (Grand Rapids: IVP Academic, 2014), 30.

who show mercy and promote peace. This meek and mild army would be a confusing force to any opposing battalion.

Jesus tells his followers if they are persecuted, they should turn the other cheek and forgive their enemies. He says they must love their enemies and pray for those who persecute them (5:44). Some hearers would have immediately thought of the subjugation they suffered at the hands of Roman rulers. Jesus says, "Don't revolt and riot. Rather, love them."

Jesus also instructs his followers that if their enemy forces them to help for one mile, they should go two miles (5:41). Roman soldiers could enlist people for temporary service without pay. Jews especially recoiled at this service. It reminded them they were under foreign rule. Yet Jesus encourages ungrudging, generous, and plentiful compliance. The army of followers Jesus forms would have been hardly recognizable to an opposing force.

He also tells his followers not to act like Zealots, a group advocating insurrection against the Romans. All who take up the sword will die by the sword (Matt. 26:52). For Jesus, enemy love, non-retaliation, and peacemaking are not just end-time ethics, but present-day conduct. Jesus practiced these virtues on earth and directed his followers to walk in his footsteps.

Jesus was forming a kingdom, an army of followers. Yet this army was unlike any army before or since. They could work for Caesar. They were to love their enemies, go the extra mile, be peacemakers, and be compliant. The armed forces Jesus trained were not of this world. We may never shoot the artillery, but we are in the Lord's army.

Death and Taxes

Jesus didn't speak explicitly on a lot of topics. He didn't mention homosexuality. He didn't speak about whether our pets go to heaven. And he didn't indicate how much one should exercise or even when someone should pray. This doesn't mean he didn't care about these topics.

However, did you know that Jesus directly addressed whether Christians should pay taxes?

Two groups come to Jesus (Mark 12:13–17). Both the Pharisees and Herodians ask him, "Should we pay taxes (*census*) to Caesar, or not?" This is an interesting coalition. The Pharisees were a populist movement who shunned Greek influence. On the other hand, the Herodians were compromisers and collaborators, the face of Roman rule.

This background helps readers see the trap laid for Jesus. The Herodians were loyal to Herod and Caesar. They interpreted refusing to pay Caesar as tantamount to rebellion. On the other side are the freedom fighters, the Pharisees. They hated the tax because it reminded them of their subjugation to Rome.

Will Jesus reveal himself as a fraud or a revolutionary? The trap is set; the bait is on the hook. Now they can watch Jesus tie himself up in his own words. But Jesus escapes their trap like a bird.

When the question is posed, Jesus asks for a denarius. A denarius was a Roman silver coin bearing the bust of Tiberius Caesar (AD 14–37). On it was an abbreviated Latin inscription, *Tiberius Caesar Divi Augusti Filius Augustus*, which can be translated as "Tiberius Caesar Augustus, Son of the Divine Augustus."

The reverse side bore an image of Tiberius's mother, Livia, and the inscription, *Pontifex Maximus* (High Priest).

Jesus looks at the denarius and asks, "Whose image and inscription is this?" They reply, "Caesar's." Jesus then gives his famous cryptic answer: "Give to Caesar the things that are Caesar's, and to God the things that are God's" (Mark 12:17). Though it may seem like a simple answer, there are many interpretations of Jesus's statement.

The most common way of viewing Jesus's answer is a *pro-empire* reading. Most see Jesus as supporting a division between religion and politics. In this view, the government has an uncontested sphere of power that Jesus acknowledges. Jesus is concerned with a spiritual kingdom, while Caesar is after an earthly kingdom. Caesar owns that which belongs to the state. God owns that which belongs to the kingdom of God. Therefore, people can give taxes to Caesar and serve God. The two are not opposed.

However, several problems arise with this view. First, it is hard to reconcile this with the typical Jewish view of the day. Jews would not accept the division between religion and politics. Second, this view tends to be anachronistic, fitting too neatly into the American ideal of separating church and state. Finally, if Jesus was simply supporting paying taxes to Caesar, then the amazement of the Pharisees doesn't make sense (12:17). The trap was set up so that a clear answer affirming either side would have raised the ire of the other. Jesus's answer is subtle, and so our interpretation must capture his sophistication.

Because of these problems, others interpret Jesus's statement as *anti-empire*. Essentially, Jesus's answer pitted God's authority against Caesar's. When Jesus mentioned the "image" of Caesar, every Jewish mind would run to Genesis and remember that humans are made in the image of God (Gen. 1:26). The "image" of Caesar reminds them Caesar is under God's authority.

Then when Jesus says, "Give to God the things that are God's," a Jew would recognize God as the exclusive Lord and master of all. He is their sole king, and therefore all things belong to God. The implications for Caesar, then, are obvious. Jesus reasserts a typical Jewish worldview. No imperial ruler, not even Caesar, has any claim on the Israelites. God is their only true king and master.

The biggest problem with this interpretation is similar to the one above. If this is Jesus's response, then the Herodians should be fuming and claiming rebellion. Instead, both groups are utterly amazed and befuddled (12:17). Jesus escaped their trap. He affirmed neither view.

The confusion of the Pharisees and Herodians indicates a mediating reply from Jesus. Jesus does not *pit* God's authority against Caesar. Nor does he *separate* their authority. He *sources* Caesar's authority in God's and *subordinates* Caesar's authority under God's. Jesus disagrees with both the Pharisees and Herodians.

God's reign subsumes Caesar's, but there is overlap. Jesus is not a typical revolutionary. By replying they can "give to Caesar what is Caesar's," Jesus affirms the legitimacy of government, despite its problems. But Jesus does not stop here. He continues by answering more than they asked.

They ask whether they should pay taxes to Caesar, and he responds with what they should give to God. All things belong to God. By giving them more than they asked, Jesus affirms God is superior to Caesar.

Let me state this very clearly: Jesus's answer *cannot* be construed to mean these are separate spheres (political/religious). His answer both brings the two rules together and institutionally distinguishes between them. God has all authority, and Caesar's fits under God's—not over it.

Therefore, there is no contradiction in giving Caesar what is Caesar's, because ultimately it is all God's. We owe everything to God, and God says to give some to Caesar. While God and Caesar both have authority, there is a radical difference in their kinds of authority. God's authority *appoints* Caesar's authority.

> **God has all authority, and Caesar's fits under God's—not over it.**

This means God's people can *submit* to Caesar (give to Caesar), and *subvert* Caesar (give to God all things) at the same time. Caesar's authority is limited. God's is unlimited. Caesar's rule is temporal. God's rule is eternal. Caesar's reign is narrow. God's reign is comprehensive and sovereign over Caesar's reign.

Jesus's message was subversive, but it was subversive by being submissive to God. Jesus follows the way of the dove.

Jesus's Innocence Before Pilate

Jesus's dove-like way is also showcased in his innocence before Pilate. Jesus's political message brings him before a Roman governor (Mark 15:1–15). Pilate asks him, "Are you the King of the Jews?" It's a political question.

This charge of being King of the Jews was a hot topic at the time. Revolution was in the air. Before Jesus's time, under Greek rule, a family called the Maccabees led a revolt that cleansed and rededicated the temple (164 BC). During the time of Jesus, Judas the Galilean led a rebellion against Rome because Quirinius (6 BC) imposed a census for Roman taxation. After Jesus, the Sicarii (dagger men) stirred up revolutionary fervor, which inspired the Zealots to wage war against Rome (AD 68–70).

Pilate himself had tried to bring Roman law into Jerusalem but backed down after a mass protest. One time, fearing a riot, he sent troops to kill Galileans who were offering sacrifices. He captured and condemned Barabbas, a leader of a murderous uprising.

This is the background behind the question, "Are you the King of the Jews?" Jesus replies, "My kingdom is not of this world. . . . If my kingdom were of this world, my servants would fight, so that I wouldn't be handed over to the Jews. But as it is, my kingdom is not from here" (John 18:36).

For many, Jesus's statement confirms Jesus was only interested in building a spiritual kingdom, a reign in the hearts of mankind. Pilate has no reason to fear.

But this can't be right. This interpretation doesn't fit the hope prophesied in the Old Testament. There is nothing about a heavenly, disembodied, and spiritual kingdom in the Old Testament prophecies, nor in Jesus's own ministry.

Therefore, we must ask again what Jesus meant by this statement that his kingdom is not *of* this world. We must be careful to notice what Jesus does *not* say. He does not deny being a king. He does not say the world is not the sphere of his kingdom. He does not deny a political revolution.

By saying his kingdom is not "of this world," Jesus affirms his kingdom has a different *source, nature,* and *means.* Jesus is not sidestepping politics; he is asserting a different kind of politic. His kingdom doesn't follow earthly rules. Its character is otherworldly. It won't come as or when they expect. His kingdom is unique.

Jesus's following statement confirms this interpretation. If his kingdom were of this world, his servants would fight (John 18:36). Had Jesus been interested in a typical kingdom, his first task would have been to recruit soldiers.

In one sense, Jesus poses no threat against the Empire. But this doesn't mean his kingdom is not active in this world, or that it has nothing to do with this world. Jesus's kingdom is still *coming.*

Pilate doesn't know what to do with the way of the dove. He recognizes Jesus's innocence. Matthew says Pilate washed his hands of Jesus's blood (Matt. 27:24). This critical moment should cause readers to pause. A Roman governor who fears insurrection, to the point of imprisoning Barabbas, is convinced of Jesus's innocence. Jesus is not a Zealot. When Jesus stands in front of Pilate, Pilate doesn't see an insurrectionist.

> By sending Jesus to his death, Pilate seals the fate of all earthly kingdoms. In crucifying the King of the Jews, Pilate enthrones him.

Pilate fears the crowd, so he offers to release Barabbas and crucify Jesus. The irony is potent. The *true* insurrectionist is set free, while the prince of peace is crucified.

But the irony goes deeper. Barabbas and his rebellion won't make a dent in Rome's armor. However, by sending Jesus to his death, Pilate seals the fate of all earthly kingdoms. In crucifying the King of the Jews, Pilate enthrones him. Let's look at his coronation.

A Roman Triumph

Have you ever considered that a cross, rather than a stone, stands at the center of our faith? If Jesus had been condemned as a blasphemer according to Jewish law, he would have been stoned. Crucifixion was a Roman punishment, not a Jewish one.

At the cross we learn how Jesus interacted with Roman rule. The cross ought to be the center of our political theology, the foundation upon which we build.[3]

Jesus's passion narrative bursts with political imagery and implications. His entrance into Jerusalem is his death parade. Yet for those with eyes to see, it is also Jesus's Roman triumph.

A Roman triumph is a well-known event, amply documented in history. It was a parade that functioned to honor and celebrate a victorious Roman general or emperor for military success. In these parades, a triumphing general had god-like status for a day.[4] These ceremonies are similar to the parades thrown for soldiers and generals returning to America.

In Rome, military heroes were called triumphators. The triumphator would dress in kingly garb (sometimes purple), have a laurel

[3] Oscar Cullmann put it this way: "The cross of Christ should lead the church in all its deliberations about the relationship of church and state; not just in its negative aspects, but in its positive aspects as well." Oscar Cullmann, *The State in the New Testament* (New York: Charles Scribner's Sons, 1956), 7.

[4] The following details come mainly from Zonaras, *Epitome* 7.21. See also Adam Winn, *Reading Mark's Christology under Caesar: Jesus the Messiah and Roman Imperial Ideology* (Downers Grove, IVP Academic, 2018), 157–62.

placed on his head, and hold a branch in his right hand. The triumphator would mount a chariot and others would march beside him.

A bull, designated for sacrifice, was also in the procession. Next
to the bull walked a Roman official who carried a double-bladed
ax over his shoulders. The animal trudged next to the weapon that
would end its life.

Upon entering the city, he was escorted to the Roman Forum.
He would ride up to the Capitol. Here he performed rites and
made offerings. He would be offered wine, but customarily refused
it. Then, the bull was sacrificed. At the end of the ceremony, the
triumphator was often elevated above the ground. Sometimes they
were elevated alone, but many examples exist where they were
flanked by two people, one on either side. When evening came, he
would be escorted home, accompanied by flutes and pipes.

If we look through the lens of a Roman triumph, we see Jesus's
road to the cross under a new political script.

Jesus is led by the soldier inside the palace, the *praetorium*
(Mark 15:16). The praetorium is the Roman military headquarters,
but also a word that described the bodyguard of the emperor who
would have been present at a Roman triumph.

At the praetorium a whole battalion of Roman soldiers gathers
(15:16). The battalion would have been a military unit numbering
600 soldiers. These soldiers adorn Jesus with a purple garment and
a crown of thorns. They then mock Jesus as the King of the Jews
and strike him with a reed (a fake scepter), spit on him (rather than
kissing his feet), and kneel.

When they lead Jesus out, they compel Simon of Cyrene to
carry his cross. This mirrors the Roman official who carried a
double-bladed ax over his shoulder, ready to slay the bull. Then

they lead Jesus to Golgotha, the place of the skull (15:22). They offer Jesus wine, but he refuses (15:23). Then they perform their own ritual sacrifice. They elevate the triumphator through crucifixion, lifting him up between two robbers. Above him they place a sign that reads, "The King of the Jews" (15:24–27).

Those who passed by him didn't praise him. Instead, they derided him and made fun of his impotence. He couldn't even save himself (15:29–32). However, he was the only one to travel this path who would defeat mortality. Darkness covered the whole land—an augural sign. Jesus uttered a loud cry and breathed his last.

To cap it off, a centurion recognized what had happened. He would have been very familiar with the proceedings of a Roman triumph. The one who pledged loyalty to Caesar, declaring the triumphal emperor the son of God, looked upon Jesus's battered, bloody, and dead body. Astonishingly, he declared, "*This* man was the Son of God" (15:39, emphasis added).

Christ's Passion as a Roman Triumph	
Praetorian (Mark 15:16)	Roman military headquarters, but also a word that described the personal bodyguard of the emperor who would have been present at a Roman triumph.
Cohort of Roman Soldiers (Mark 15:16)	Military unit numbering 600 soldiers parallels the soldiers marching with the triumphator.
Adorned with Purple Garment (Mark 15:17)	The Roman triumphator would have been adorned in a purple garment.

Mock Praise (Mark 15:18–19)	Soldiers saluted, recognized his position, and prostrated themselves. This was an inversion of the homage Roman soldiers paid to the triumphator.
Simon of Cyrene (Mark 15:21)	In a triumph, the bull that was to be sacrificed was led in the procession. Next to the bull walked a Roman official who carried a double-bladed ax, ready to kill the bull.
Wine Mixed with Myrrh (Mark 15:23)	At the end of the Roman procession the triumphator would have been offered wine, which he would have refused.
Two Thieves (Mark 15:27)	At the end of a Roman triumph, the triumphator was often elevated above the ground. Sometimes they were alone, but many examples exist where they were flanked by two people, one on the right and one on the left.
Confession (Mark 15:39)	The centurion recognized the "triumph" Jesus received at the hands of the Roman soldiers and declared him to be King.

The point of all this is that Jesus's death is his kingly enthrone-ment. However, it is painted in the garb of a Roman triumph. Jesus's kingdom is fully political. But it comes through submission and sacrifice. In the *pivotal* moment of Jesus's life, he submits to the Roman eagle as a dove, but conquers the eagle by being a dove.

Conclusion

This chapter has held in tension Jesus's political kingdom announcement and actions with the ethics of the dove. Jesus's subversion and submission come together. Jesus and his disciples were not anarchists or insurrectionists. They did not seek to overthrow Caesar.

That is because Jesus's kingdom is of the Spirit. The Spirit comes on gentle wings; Caesar conquers with brutal weapons. Jesus's politic was of a different order and was to be manifested in the weak rather than the strong.

When we come to the Bible, we tend to separate religion and politics, the earthly and spiritual, the private and public. Jesus comes and blows up all our paradigms. His message was political and even subversive, but he also taught the way of the dove: enemy love, non-retaliation, submission, and sacrifice.

We can affirm both because Jesus's kingdom is of another nature. It is both here and not here. It is both present and coming.

It is these tensions we must live out.

CHAPTER 3

Reimagining Politics with Jesus

Submission and Subversion in the Modern World

It was getting heated. In a number of ways.

In November of 2019, some family and friends were sitting outside in San Diego. The rooftop restaurant was close to the beach, and we were all enjoying the warm weather. The sun was beating down on us, but it wasn't the only source of heat. We had started talking about what to do considering the recent racial tension.

I argued that we don't understand what it's like to start "behind," so we need compassion and empathy. We need to think of how we can be agents of change. As an analogy, I compared life to a game where people in different social situations step onto the court already down twenty—the score doesn't begin at zero. Some were arguing in response, saying money won't fix the problem. I kept contending we need to do *something*.

One person fired a sharp retort at me. So I accused this person of being whipped by far-right podcasts. Big mistake. That only fueled the fire. I am no stranger to impassioned arguments. I have theological disagreements almost every day in class. But this one was getting a little out of hand. Tensions rose, and we both said things we regretted.

Anger reveals our loyalties, whether we admit it or not. If we have fractured relationships because of politics, we need to ask whether we are placing too much hope in political promises.

This event is not unique. It seems to be happening to more and more people. Close relationships are suddenly torn apart by political disagreements. Many people avoid the topic to keep the peace, but others have embraced the conflict and bulldozed plenty of their friends in the process.

Nationalism or Nonconformity

With all the frustration and confusion, we are tempted to turn toward one of two extremes in terms of political engagement: *nationalism* or *nonconformity*. Either we combine our Christian hope with the state, or we avoid politics altogether.

Christian nationalism manifests itself in thinking the rule of God and the government's authority are closely aligned. Our nation's story becomes a central piece of the redemptive story. It is patriotism taken to the extreme.

Both political parties in America can fall into nationalistic thinking. In December 2020, there was an event called the Jericho March in Washington, DC. It was a pro-Trump rally by Christians who believed the election had been stolen. Of course, Jericho alludes to the biblical story of the Israelites marching around the city until the walls fell. According to reports, there was language like, "Trump is God's instrument!" and "Opposing Trump's re-election is Satanic!"

The other side follows similar moves. Many progressive Christians condemn the policies of the religious right because they don't prioritize the Christian values of Jesus—non-retaliation, caring for the marginalized, etc. So, when the right opposes social safety nets, generous immigration policies, or redistribution of wealth, the left rises up, declaring their party represents God's decrees.

Many grow frustrated when they see people equating Christianity with the nation we reside in, so they respond with *non-conformity*. In this view, religion and politics should not be mixed, because politics is a public reality, and religion is a private reality. They say the church should have nothing to do with politics. (Remember—we already saw how *the gospel of the kingdom* corrects this way of thinking.)

This creates separatism, a monastery mindset. In some evangelical churches nothing is said from the pulpit about politics because "that is an issue of the world." We are advocates for God's kingdom, and that reign is manifested in our hearts. Therefore, they argue, we should withdraw from politics and work toward the new heavens and earth.

Christians and Politics

Option 1 ——————— Faithfulness ——————— Option 2

Non-conformity ——— Citizenship ——————— Nationalism

Neither nationalism nor nonconformity represents Jesus's stance toward governing authorities. This chapter sets some guiding principles for how we can live out our political gospel and public witness. Some might be frustrated by the lack of specific direction on policies, but I think this frustration reveals part of the problem.

Typically, political "discipleship" is being told what to think about certain *issues* (abortion, immigration, climate change) rather than beginning with the foundational principles of political theology. This is backwards. We have to work *up* from the foundation rather than *down* from the issues.

God's Servant, Therefore Honor

The first thing we can assert based on Jesus's ministry is that we should view governing authorities as God's servant. When Jesus was asked whether people should pay taxes to Caesar, he said they should *because* the emperor's authority comes from God.[1]

Governments come from God. Governments don't exist, first and foremost, because we have made a social contract, or elected a ruler, or because they control the army and police, or because of economic factors. They exist because God has established them to promote the common good (order, justice, virtue, and peace). This means we should honor them.

> We should view governing authorities as God's servant.

---

[1] David VanDrunen, *Politics after Christendom: Political Theology in a Fractured World* (Grand Rapids: Zondervan Academic, 2020), 25–32.

No matter how corrupt and off-putting, earthly rulers are God's servants. Cyrus, the king of Persia, was even called God's messianic figure (Isa. 45:1). Honoring them challenges the political posture of nonconformity (1 Tim. 2:1–4).

But viewing rulers as God's servants is difficult for us because Americans struggle with an anti-authoritarian attitude. When the "other party" is in office, we get whipped into a frenzy. We think the world is ending. Turns out, we're all nonconformists when the *other* guy is in power.

So, if governing authorities are God's servants, what does it look like to honor and obey in the modern era?

Though Jesus had every opportunity to be critical of Rome, he rarely did so explicitly. When asked pointedly what to do with Rome, he said to obey them and pay taxes. Americans tend to have a critical attitude toward politics, but Christians must show the way of the dove.

Sometimes when a president is elected in America, people who oppose the individual begin using the phrase #NotMyPresident. At one level, this may be a simple way to voice frustration and critique, but I think people mean more than that. They are saying he is not their president, they will not submit to him, and they will not recognize his rule. This is not how Jesus spoke of Caesar.

> Americans have much to be thankful for, no matter who is in power.

Even though we will always have critiques of the authorities, and so did Jesus, we can speak of the good they do and honor them, knowing God put them there. We can encourage those in our congregations who work for the state. We can send thank-you cards to our senators and police officers. The Scriptures affirm the organization and governing of a people as a good thing. Americans have much to be thankful for, no matter who is in power.

In church and at home, it would be wise to pray for governing authorities of both parties. This shows how the church is seeking the good of the city and teaches your children that you believe government is a gift from God. We could do more to create a culture of respecting governing authorities. Many of us have some repentance to do on this front.

It also means if our authorities ask us to do things, we should comply unless it goes explicitly against our faith. This became a complicated issue in 2020–21 during the COVID-19 pandemic. Churches were told they could not meet or only meet in a limited fashion. Christians struggled with scriptural commands that seemed at odds: loving one's neighbor (Mark 12:31), not neglecting to meet together (Heb. 10:25), and submitting to governing authorities (Rom. 13:1).

Part of the reason it was so difficult was because the public health issue did fall under the government's jurisdiction, but it also conflicted with a command in the Scriptures to meet. There was overlap in authority structures, and Christians disagreed about what to do. Lest you think this is a once-in-a-lifetime anomaly, this will not be the last time we encounter a situation that requires thought and prayer.

No matter what one decides on that issue, Christians should imitate the posture of Jesus toward the ruling elite. He honored governing authorities. If this is not your first instinct concerning the government, then you should examine how "biblical" your political formation has become.

Not Ultimate, Therefore Don't Rely

The life of Jesus also shows us that civil government and governing authorities are legitimate, but they are not ultimate.

The problem with most political theology is imbalance. Asserting government is God's servant is not enough. We also must affirm the government fits within a higher sphere of authority. We have a vertical authority (God) which is primary, and horizontal authorities which are secondary. Jesus affirmed the state's legitimacy, but also demoted them.

Only affirming the government as God's servant without subordinating it to God's Word will leave us out of balance. Jesus never said, "There is no place like Rome." Rome *crucified* him. He did not place his hope in Rome's rule.

Jesus was following the tradition of the Old Testament. The kings of the earth fought against Abraham (Gen. 14). Pharaoh opposed and enslaved God's people (Exod. 1–2). Canaanite kings warred against Israel (Num. 21). The king of Moab tried to curse God's people (Num. 23). The king of Assyria and Babylon exiled God's people.

David says the kings of the earth take their stand against the Lord and his people (Ps. 2:2). He tells God's assembly not to put their trust in nobles or human beings who cannot save them. Psalm 146:3–10 is worth quoting here:

> Do not trust in nobles,
> in a son of man, who cannot save.

When his breath leaves him,
he returns to the ground;
on that day his plans die.

Happy is the one whose help is the God of Jacob,
whose hope is in the LORD his God,
the Maker of heaven and earth,
the sea and everything in them.
He remains faithful forever,
executing justice for the exploited
and giving food to the hungry.
The LORD frees prisoners.
The LORD opens the eyes of the blind.
The LORD raises up those who are oppressed.
The LORD loves the righteous.
The LORD protects resident aliens
and helps the fatherless and the widow,
but he frustrates the ways of the wicked.

The LORD reigns forever;
Zion, your God reigns for all generations.

In the same way, we must recognize governing authorities are not ultimate. They will *not* establish justice. They will *not* help the fatherless and the widow. They will *not* frustrate the way of the wicked. They will not do these things in an ultimate sense.

Earthly kingdoms will come and go. Only God's kingdom will endure forever and bring true justice. Viewing the civil magistrates as ultimate manifests itself in obsession over their rule.

There's no American Savior. Only a Jewish one.

And in America, currently, this obsession with partisanship is killing Christian witness. Too many of us are so wrapped in the fight that we panic when our chosen politician is not elected. A steady diet of political propaganda from our partisan networks and podcasts will not conform us to the image of Christ.

Politics matter. But news media exist to make money, which means getting your attention so you'll come back tomorrow. Fear and outrage are addicting, and both the left and the right know how to get you hooked.

The American church is dangerously close to Israel, who built and worshipped other idols on their hills, all the while continually going to the Jerusalem temple. "Religious belief" has not been replaced with "partisan belief," but combined with it.

American politics is another religion, and people define themselves as right or left. Both political sides have their founding myth

> Only God's kingdom will endure forever and bring true justice.

(1619 or 1776), their patriarchs (FDR or Reagan), their prophets (Maddow or Shapiro), and their scriptures (the Constitution, but interpreted differently). Both have forms of membership (how to vote and talk like the rest of the party), excommunication (cancel culture), and penance (reparations). Both insist they are faithful to the "American Dream" and that the other side betrays it.

Our leaders are viewed as secular priests, even though we would never say it aloud. They sit in rooms of power. They have special access. We gather to hear what they have to say. We hang on their every word. We become obsessed.

When Ruth Bader Ginsburg died in September of 2020, groups of mourners gathered outside the Supreme Court. Some knelt, others prayed, others held candles. The steps of the Supreme Court had become the American Western Wall.[2]

But the Scriptures put the governing authorities in their proper positions. They will not usher in the new creation. They will not bring lasting peace. They will not bring long-term life, liberty, or happiness. Only God will do this.

Jesus announced another kingdom was present amid these kingdoms. We serve another king. "This means that no affection we may feel toward a political tribe should compare to our allegiance toward Christ's heavenly kingdom."[3] We are united under another king, no matter our political differences.

Accountable, Therefore Reform

The non-ultimacy of the governing authorities leads to a final point. If they are accountable to God, and if they only have a certain sphere of authority, they can be critiqued, subverted, and reformed.

Since God has ordained these magistrates, they have a task. Civil officials are under a higher authority. They are servants and delegates. They don't demarcate their role or define the good. Rather, they recognize what is good and legislate it. The problem is that they often misidentify the good, step outside of their sphere of authority, and begin to call their citizens to false worship.

This is why we can affirm the government's legitimacy and also affirm Jesus's politically subversive message. He announces the victory of his kingdom. He says the Gentile rulers are tyrants. He claims their titles. He attacks the Legion because they are warping his good creation. Rome perpetrates evil; it no longer promotes the good.

Extensive evidence exists of Rome's exploitation. Though they sought to spread peace, they left a wake of death. Romans were terribly violent in war, killing, raping, and pillaging. Their forms of execution included sewing people inside animals, burying people alive, and crucifying them.

But Rome is not alone.

America (and all other nations) shows evidence of deep corruption as well. Her history rests on black slaves. Their families were ripped apart, and America's economy was built on their scarred backs. Even after slaves were set free, there have been segregation, redlining, police brutality, and general distrust.

America still murders their helpless. Since the ruling of *Roe v. Wade* in 1973, there have been more than 61 million abortions in the United States. This is despite the fact that scientific advancements have both proven the humanity of babies at an earlier stage and made children viable earlier in pregnancy than ever before. Technology has provided the public with unprecedented awareness of the reality of abortion. But we slice and dice our way through our children anyway.

America also continues to sell sex, which distorts and destroys marriages and feeds sex slavery. The amount of pornography consumed in America is staggering, and must be factored into the rise of sexual abuse cases.

Being the Kingdom of God

So, what should we do? March? Protest? Overthrow? Stock up on ammunition?

The most subversive thing we can do is exist as the kingdom of God amid the kingdom of man.

This was Jesus's main political action. He came announcing a new way and forming a new community. We, too, witness to the world about the King and his kingdom where justice, peace, and harmony reside. Jesus didn't seek to change the structures around him. He preached another politic, another way.

And this alternative politic is manifested where? In the community of believers we call the church.

That is one reason it is so important to be a part of a local church and around other Christians who remind you of your true loyalty and the kingdom to come. Whenever a preacher preaches, he makes a political speech, reminding you that Jesus is King in the present. Whenever you receive communion, you re-pledge your allegiance to Christ's kingdom. And whenever you share the gospel of Christ with a neighbor, friend, or family member, you are helping advance Christ's campaign among the nations.

For a Christian, the political life must begin inside the church.

Though this might sound like "standard Christian advice," it is of utmost importance. The local church is the political rallying point for all of God's people. We all occupy different stations, but we are all politicians.

Stay-at-home moms might wonder what the "political gospel" has to do with them. In training their kids to love the heavenly King, they are the first specialists for a new heavenly citizen. Businessmen and women are ambassadors for a new regime behind enemy lines. Artists and creatives provide symbols and images for a new kingdom. Musicians craft songs and liturgy that form our desires and imaginations for a new city. Teachers and students are training for a life of influence under the reign of their Sovereign.

Our primary subversive political witness is to create a community that is loyal to King Jesus and make all other political allegiances pale in comparison. A political gospel subordinates all other tribal instincts. And this will have a leavening effect upon society.

Doing Good for All

However, there are also secondary things we can do. Jesus didn't navel-gaze; he also cared about the suffering of humanity in society. While New Testament Christians had no opportunity to reform the system, we live in a different political era.

Civil government is accountable to God for its misdeeds and mismanagement. Its legitimacy is based on promoting justice, rewarding the good, and punishing the evil. When it ceases to do this, we must confront it with its God-given purpose again.

So, what does it mean to subvert and reform the state in the modern era? There are different forms of rebellion, but we must define what it doesn't mean. Jesus explicitly said his kingdom was not of this world. If it were, his servants would fight (John 18:36).

Rebellion, therefore, doesn't mean storming the Capitol like those who did on January 6, 2021. It doesn't mean looting like

72   POLITICAL GOSPEL

those who did after George Floyd's death. We advocate for the end
of abortion, but we don't kill doctors who perform abortions. We
march and protest, but we don't form mobs of destruction. We
work to elect candidates of integrity and conviction, but we don't
harass public officials at town halls or school board meetings.

When Jesus was arrested, his disciples asked, "Lord, should we
strike with the sword?" (Luke 22:49). Then Peter struck the high
priest's servant and cut off his right ear. But Jesus said, "Put your
sword back in its place because all who take up the sword will per-
ish by the sword" (Matt. 26:52). So we see subversion doesn't mean
violence.

According to the biblical tradition, what does it mean?
Christopher Bryan says it well: "The biblical tradition subverts
human order . . . by consistently confronting its representatives
with the truth about its origin and its purpose."[4] We know where
governments derive their authority (God), what their task is (judgment), and how far their authority extends (limited). Therefore, we
have a unique prophetic ability to hold our rulers' feet to the fire.

Jesus subverted the state by speaking the truth and enacting
justice. In Mark 5, Jesus doesn't fail to be prophetic by bringing to
light the true identity of the demons. We also can call by name the
policies, officials, events, and worldviews that oppress people if we
have the opportunity. As Hendricks says:

> We must call by name tax laws that favor the inter-
> ests of the rich.

---

[4] Christopher Bryan, *Render to Caesar: Jesus, the Early Church, and the Roman
Superpower* (New York: Oxford University Press, 2005), 125.

We must call by name corporate boards that underpay workers.

We must call by name totalitarian states that redefine sexuality.

We must call by name public officials who serve the privileged few.

We must call by name ministers who exploit those they claim to serve.

We must call by name prosperity preachers who pervert God's people.

We must call by name worldviews that redefine the family.

We must call by name policies that denigrate certain groups of humanity.[5]

But Jesus doesn't stop there. He declares *and enacts* a new kingdom: word *and* deed. He exorcises the demons and brings the demon-possessed man to a new social position: from death to life. We must declare *and enact* this alternate way of life as well. We enact this as we do good to others and seek their welfare above our own.

---

[5] Obery M. Hendricks Jr., *The Politics of Jesus: Rediscovering the True Revolutionary Nature of Jesus's Teachings and How They Have Been Corrupted* (New York: Three Leaves, 2007), 268–69. These come from Hendricks, but I adapted them.

There is a place for civil disobedience and reform. The exorcism of the demoniac and Jesus's anger at the money changers in
the temple shows that, especially when dehumanization occurs, we
arise. This is what happened in the Civil Rights Movement.

Martin Luther King Jr. helped lead a boycott of downtown businesses in protest of segregation. He was arrested in Birmingham,
where he penned "Letter from a Birmingham Jail." As King noted,
the critique will always be that these activities are unwise, rash,
foolish, and reckless. But this is what King said in response to other
Christian leaders who were criticizing the movement.

> While confined here in the Birmingham city jail,
> I came across your recent statement calling my
> present activities "unwise and untimely." . . . I am
> in Birmingham because injustice is here. Just as
> the prophets of the eighth century B.C. left their
> villages and carried their "thus saith the Lord" far
> beyond the boundaries of their home towns, and
> just as the Apostle Paul left his village of Tarsus and
> carried the gospel of Jesus Christ to the far corners
> of the Greco Roman world, so am I compelled to
> carry the gospel of freedom beyond my own home
> town. Like Paul, I must constantly respond to the
> Macedonian call for aid. . . .
>
> We know through painful experience that free-
> dom is never voluntarily given by the oppressor; it
> must be demanded by the oppressed. Frankly, I
> have yet to engage in a direct action campaign that
> was "well timed" in the view of those who have

not suffered unduly from the disease of segregation. For years now I have heard the word "Wait!"
It rings in the ear of every Negro with piercing
familiarity. This "Wait" has almost always meant
"Never." We must come to see, with one of our
distinguished jurists, that "justice too long delayed
is justice denied."[6]

In the late summer of 1963, 200,000 marchers went to
Washington, DC, where King delivered his "I Have a Dream"
speech. In 1964, MLK stood directly behind Lyndon B. Johnson
as he signed into existence the Equal Employment Opportunity
Commission, which authorized the federal government to enforce
desegregation and prevented other forms of discrimination.

When things failed to improve, people marched. King said the
marches were the voice of the oppressed rising up in the tradition of
Jesus. Someone who participates in civil disobedience refuses to do
what the government asks, but they at the very same time remain
under the rule of the government because they accept the consequences for their actions. Martin Luther King Jr. said it this way:

> One may well ask: "How can you advocate break-
> ing some laws and obeying others?" The answer
> lies in the fact that there are two types of laws: just
> and unjust. I would be the first to advocate obey-
> ing just laws. One has not only a legal but a moral
> responsibility to obey just laws. Conversely, one

---

[6] Martin Luther King Jr., "Letter from Birmingham Jail" (from the Estate
of Martin Luther King Jr.), https://kinginstitute.stanford.edu/sites/mlk/files
/letterfrombirmingham_wwcw_0.pdf (accessed June 30, 2021).

has a moral responsibility to disobey unjust laws. I
would agree with St. Augustine that "an unjust law
is no law at all."[7]

For King, subverting the system was aimed at the flourishing
of humanity. The goal is always the same. The circumstances determined the action.

The government is legitimate, but it is also accountable, and
we are forming citizens of another kingdom. That means our primary witness is pointing to the city to come and existing as the
kingdom of God in the city of man. We declare the politic of Jesus.

However, we can also work to help those living around us. As
citizens of another kingdom, we don't put our hope here, but it is
because of this that we can confront injustice, rebel against corrupt
rulers, and nonviolently tear down prejudiced systems. We do all of
this out of obedience to God, our true authority.

Conclusion

I met a lot of Christians who didn't want to wear masks during
the COVID-19 pandemic. One told me he would walk into Home
Depot without one, and the workers would request that he put on
a mask. He would respond, "Call the cops on me if you wish."

They never did.

Is this the way of subversion? No. This is defining our freedom more by American ideals than by God's kingdom. The mask
mandate did not discriminate; all people had to wear them. In
addition, the purpose of the mask mandate was public health, but

---

[7] King, "Letter from Birmingham Jail."

the purpose of the segregation laws was to enshrine a difference of worth and value.

The life of Jesus shows us subversion always advocates for the kingdom of God and sometimes opposes the kingdoms of the earth. Jesus recognized the state's legitimate role in ordering and enacting justice in society. Even if we disagree with the state's orders, we should comply unless they go against divine commands.

Jesus's message and actions were subversive: the way of the kingdom. But they were also submissive: the way of the dove. We tend to emphasize one or the other, but the Bible brings them together: *subversion through submission, conquest through peace, victory through suffering.*

We are not anti-government or pro-government but alter-government. We await a kingdom not of this world. This doesn't mean escapism or complete indifference to what the government does. We should not withdraw when we are losing or push forward when we are winning.

There is no winning or losing. God has won in Jesus Christ. That is the gospel.

An alter-government perspective recognizes these rulers serve under God's reign for a limited time. They can do good or evil. But their reign is limited. Their reign is limited because they are mortal. Kingdoms rise and fall, but one kingdom stands forever. It cannot be shaken.

Therefore, Christians are those that submit to and subvert the state. We do so because our kingdom is to come, but we can also hold them accountable for not rewarding the good and punishing evil. This may mean rebellion, but it might simply mean preaching a different ethic. We don't do so because we necessarily think we can transform society, but because we believe in showcasing the politics of our king.

The state will not know what to do with Christians who act like this. Like Jesus before Pilate, we might be brought before the governing authorities, but when they examine us, no charges will stand. Why? Because Christ's kingdom is not according to this world—even though it will one day encompass this world.

PART 2

POLITICAL PRESENT

CHAPTER 4

The Way of Subversion

Turning the World Upside Down

Dietrich Bonhoeffer's last words before he was hanged were these: "This is the end—for me, the beginning of life."

The Lutheran pastor and theologian was hanged before the German state in a POW camp on April 9, 1945, for defying Hitler. Bonhoeffer subverted Hitler in two ways. After Adolf Hitler became chancellor of Germany, Bonhoeffer took to the radio and denounced the ruler. The broadcast was cut off before he could finish. He lost his freedom to lecture and publish.

Bonhoeffer was eventually arrested, not for his radio broadcast, but for being involved in a plot to assassinate Hitler. What many forget is that Bonhoeffer was a committed pacificist.

He had used his contacts to spread information about a resistance movement. Bonhoeffer partnered with high-ranking German officials who placed a bomb in a briefcase at a meeting where Hitler was supposed to be. On July 20, 1944, the bomb went off. Hitler was wounded and even suffered temporary paralysis of one arm, but he lived.

Bonhoeffer understood he had a responsibility to the government, but his responsibility to God was greater. He understood that to die was to live.

Jesus, Peter, and Paul all likewise died under an oppressive government's rule. Even though we might not think much about Rome when we read the Bible, all New Testament saints lived under Caesar's shadow, and many died as rebels to the state.

When we turn to the story of the church (*political present*), the political nature of our faith remains. The subversive nature of the gospel comes into focus as Paul goes into various cities and towns. While Jesus ministered mainly in rural areas, Paul voyaged to urban centers and consistently bumped into ruling elites.

This chapter will examine our political present by looking at how the early church subverted the Empire.

The Political Allegations Against Paul

After Jesus died, how did the Empire view the Christian message? Was Rome content to let this upstart movement live at peace? Did they view the message as a challenge to their authority and way of life? Or did they consider it a blip on the radar, a few disgruntled Jews in the far reaches of Palestine not to be concerned about?

Acts gives readers a glimpse of how Rome initially received this message. One thing is clear: it was not viewed as a private message they could ignore, and it was not regarded as supporting the Caesar's sovereignty. It was "another way," a disruption, a political challenge to the Caesar's decrees.

When Paul and his companions preached, they were brought before governing authorities. Angry councils, governors, kings, mobs, merchants, and magistrates sought to quell this message. Christians were driven out of town, arrested, hauled into court, beaten, and even killed. Paul's political message destabilized the Roman world.

Subverting the Empire in Thessalonica

In this book, I have latched onto the word *subvert*. And yet, not everyone approves or appreciates the term. While I was writing this book, many people would ask me about my basic argument. When I told them, some would question whether the term *subvert* was the right one.

I pull this concept from Luke's description of Paul's ministry in Thessalonica (Acts 17). In Thessalonica, Paul preached Jesus as the Messiah. This upset the Jewish crowds, so they accused Paul of two things (17:6–7):

1. Turning the world upside down.
2. Defying the decrees of Caesar.

First, they said, "These men who have turned the world upside down have come here too." In one sense, I love this translation. I love the idea that the gospel message turns the world upside down. It fits seamlessly with the idea that the Christian message is not only political but politically subversive. However, more can be said.

The word for "turn the world upside down" can be translated differently. In Greek the term literally means "to subvert, agitate, overthrow, or disturb."

Paul is accused of subverting the world. Luke says the charges against the gospel message concern an upheaval, a cataclysm, a disruption to Rome and her way of doing things.

> The gospel message turns the world upside down.

But there is more. The text says Paul has subverted "the world" (Acts 17:6). Again, there is another way to translate this term. While "world" or "earth" is a fine translation, it can also be translated as "the Roman Empire." Luke, in fact, uses this term two times in reference to the Empire (Luke 2:1; Acts 24:5).

Therefore, Paul and his companions were accused in Thessalonica of "subverting the Roman Empire."

Some might doubt whether the above translation is warranted, but the next verse gives further substantiation. The second charge Paul's group receives is "They are all acting contrary to Caesar's decrees, saying that there is another king—Jesus" (Acts 17:7). With a statement like this, it is difficult to deny Christianity's political nature.

Luke does not define the Roman decrees Paul subverts—there could have been a number of them. The important point is this: *those in Thessalonica interpreted the claims of King Jesus as contrary to the claims of Caesar.* Paul's message is a competing scheme, a contradictory kingdom, an alternative way of life that opposed life in the Greco-Roman world.

Like his Lord, Paul was accused of subverting the Empire and defying Caesar. When Jesus came before Pilate, the Jews accused him, saying, "Anyone who makes himself king opposes Caesar" (John 19:12). A simple gospel proclamation is not just an invitation for individuals to believe in Jesus, but a politically destabilizing message.

Agitator in Philippi and Jerusalem

The accusations against Paul are not limited to Thessalonica. Other towns also make political accusations against him. In Philippi, Paul exorcises a demon from a slave girl and is charged with troubling or disturbing this Roman colony (Acts 16:16–18).[1]

This is further defined by three linked accusations (Acts 16:20): First, Paul disturbs the peace. Romans highly valued public order, and Paul and Silas disturb the *Pax Romana*.

The second accusation is linked to their Jewish identity. Paul and his followers have crossed ethnic boundaries and challenged ethnic identities.

Third, Paul is charged with declaring customs not lawful for Romans to do or practice. Those in Philippi appeal to *nationalism, ethnocentrism*, and *Roman law* in their accusations against Paul.

It is hard to conclude anything but that the gospel disrupts the fabric of Roman society. The problem in the minds of Paul's accusers is not only financial but social and political. Paul introduces new rituals based on new loyalties. Christianity was never a private

---

[1] The "Roman" flair of the Philippi episode is evident. Although Paul has visited other Roman colonies, Philippi has a particularly Roman character. Philippi is the only city designated as a "colony" (*kolōnia*) in Acts. *Kolōnia* itself is a Latin loan word (16:12). The chief officials are called "magistrates" (*stratēgos*), which is a Greek term for Roman praetors (16:35). The police are called "police," *rhabdouchos*, which are Roman officers (16:35). Finally, Paul and Silas speak of themselves as Roman citizens (16:37–38).

belief but a message that sent tremors through society. It was a public reality that got Paul thrown into jail or run out of town.

When Paul was tried before Roman governors, the accusations
continued. Paul was brought before Felix, the Roman procurator
or governor of the region. Tertullus, a skilled lawyer, accused Paul
of being an agitator and a ringleader and profaning the temple
(Acts 24:5–6).

If the first charge is accurate, Paul is a threat to the *Pax Romana*.
If the second is on target, then he is a leader of an anarchist movement. If the third is correct, Paul is a dead man, since profaning the
temple was a capital offense under Roman law.

Paul has been painted not as a mere religious prophet but a
political agitator. He has disturbed the peace with the gospel. He
must be punished; he must be silenced. Roman order depends on it.

In summary, Paul's gospel wasn't kindly received when he went
into cities. In Thessalonica, Philippi, and Jerusalem, Paul's message threatened Rome. Other cities felt the same way. In Athens,
Paul was accused of declaring foreign deities. In Corinth, Paul was
accused of persuading people to worship God contrary to the law.
In Ephesus, Paul disrupted the economy.

Accusations Against Paul in Acts			
City	**Accusation**	**Accusers**	**Verses**
Philippi	Corrupting Roman customs	Slave owners (Gentiles)	16:20–21
Thessalonica	Subverting the Empire/defying Caesar	Jews	17:6–7

Athens	Declaring foreign deities	Philosophers (Gentiles)	17:18
Corinth	Worshipping against the law	Jews	18:13
Ephesus	Economic disrupter	Shrine makers (Gentiles)	19:25–27
Jerusalem	Social agitator	Tertullus, Sanhedrin	21:27–28

Paul's message of Jesus as the rightful king sent agitations through the Empire. It was not a private message that would illicit a "Nice for you." It was not a message people could ignore. It was not a message people could shrug off. It was a message that sent Paul and his companions to prison, to the courtroom, and got them run out of town.

Paul's gospel—like that of his master and Lord—was a political message.

> **Paul's gospel—like that of his master and Lord—was a political message.**

Paul's Political Community

If we were to survey modern Christians about how they thought of their church, most (if they like their church!) would use terms that speak to the down-to-earth nature of it. They love their church because they find community there. We are happy to describe our churches with warm terms: fellowship, community, and unity.

We don't want stuffy, cold, or institutional churches. We become skittish about adding formal or political elements to our gatherings. The consistent drumbeat we hear is less institution, more community. Less politics, more love.

The relational turn has conquered in the evangelical church.[2] The grassroots fellowship movement has won. And much of this is good. We want our communities to feel organic, authentic, and relational, not stuffy, official, and authoritative.

But maybe we have overemphasized the relational. Maybe our political discipleship is malformed because we don't think of the church as a *political* assembly.

Paul traveled to establish churches—*ekklesia*—local assemblies devoted to Jesus. And at its core, the church is a political assembly.

The Church as a Political Assembly

The Greek word for "church" (*ekklesia*) refers to an institutional entity. Paul was not willing to be thrown into prison so people could have organic relationships and sip white chocolate mochas together. He was on a mission to form a new body politic.

For hundreds of years before the birth of the Christian church, *ekklesia* was understood as a political term.[3] An *ekklesia* was an assembly of citizens that made political and judicial decisions. It was an assembly of the city (*polis*).

An *ekklesia* is thus a legislative assembly or body. It may have its origin in a herald calling people out of their homes to meet in a public assembly. The preposition *ek* means "out of" and the verb *kaleo* means "to call." An *ekklesia* of a city would meet regularly and

[2] Jonathan Leeman, *Political Church: The Local Assembly as Embassy of Christ's Rule* (Downers Grove, IL: IVP Academic, 2016), 102.

[3] Leeman, *Political Church*, 135.

make decisions about law, official positions, and policy. In Athens, these decisions were made by a show of hands, ballot sheets, or stones.[4] It almost sounds like a Baptist church voting on the color of the carpet.

These political associations are in the Old Testament as well. In the Old Testament *ekklesia* refers to the gathering of men capable of bearing arms (Judges 20:2; 1 Sam. 17:47), a judicial gathering (Deut. 9:10; Judges 21:5), a political body (Ezra 10:8, 12; Neh. 8:2, 16), or the people of Israel collectively (Exod. 12:6).[5]

We even have some evidence in the early second century that Rome viewed the church's gatherings as political gatherings. Governor Pliny writes to Emperor Trajan requesting advice on what to do with Christians. He complains about them, saying he has even "forbidden political associations."[6] Trajan viewed church as a political assembly.

However helpful word studies are, they can only take us so far. There is also a theological reality at play here: the church is a political assembly primarily because she is ruled by the ascended Christ. She takes her orders from him. She gathers around a central political confession: Jesus is Lord.

---

[4] *New International Dictionary of the New Testament Theology and Exegesis*, ed. Willem A. VanGemeren (Grand Rapids: Zondervan, 1987), vol. 2, 135. Thucydides, *History of the Peloponnesian War* 1.87.1–2; Xenonphon, *Hellenica*. 1.7.9.

[5] Since *ekklesia* is a Greek word and the Old Testament was written in Hebrew, this word isn't in the original OT text. However, the word is used several times in the Septuagint, the Greek translation of the Old Testament completed in the second century BC.

[6] Pliny to Trajan, *Epistulae* X.96.

This is the criterion for membership in the community. The church is a people united under a common governing authority.[7] She has her own government and authority structures. Therefore, the church answers first and foremost to the voice of Christ.

As Paul says to the Philippians, your citizenship is in heaven (Phil. 3:20). Thus, the church represents Christ's rule on earth by happily living under his reign and welcoming all to do the same. Christ is her authority and administrator.

As we've already seen, Christ's reign is not merely spiritual, as some assume. He is our ultimate authority for things both earthly and spiritual. There is confusion about the political nature of the church because when it is viewed from the outside, it looks like a religious institution. There is no visible rule or source of government. That is because her ruler is Christ, who is hidden in heaven.

Jesus's citizens reinforce their identity by meeting together, reminding one another of their true allegiance. This includes worship. When you go to church on Sunday and sing songs, it is not merely because the pastor couldn't think of anything else to do. Worship is a political act. It is a declaration, a reaffirmation of a covenant ceremony, an embodied act of submission to the Lord, an act of honor to the one to whom all honor is due. We raise our voices and arms in praise because we have one king, one shepherd. It is our declaration of loyalty to him and him alone.

Churches also have a law code and narrative that direct their actions. It is not the law of the state, but the Scriptures. The Bible is the rule of law given by the monarch to his subjects. Sin, in this

[7] Leeman, *Political Church*, 114.

way, is anarchy and treason, disobedience to God's law and rebellion against the King.

So how did the early church act as the army of Christ? How did she welcome new citizens and maintain their identity? For this reality, we turn to the visible practices of the church.

Political Sacraments

Social groups have various ways of maintaining and reminding themselves of their identities. Sports teams have jerseys, banners, chants, and songs. Armies have flags, uniforms, confessions, marching melodies, and gatherings. America has sacred days, songs, and memorabilia.

In the same way, the church has rituals. In worship gatherings, two specific rituals—commonly called sacraments or ordinances—not only glorify and honor Christ, but further the political and counter-cultural message that Christians promote.

Jesus instituted two signs to mark his community: baptism and the Lord's Supper. Both signs make invisible grace visible, but they are much more than that.

Remember the word filing thing we talked about earlier? Just like the words *gospel*, *kingdom*, and *faith*, we tend to file the word *sacrament* as a religious term. That is certainly what it has become. However, the original context is, once again, political.

Julius Caesar is the first person recorded in history as using a sacramentum in a military context. He described it as a voluntary oath taken by soldiers entering the Roman army, a visible sign of an invisible reality.[8] The Roman historian Livy says a sacramentum was a soldier's oath of obedience.[9] Tacitus also referred to the term as a verbal pledge of allegiance a soldier gives to his emperor.[10] Suetonius writes that all military personnel serving Rome were "bound by the sacrament" or oath of fidelity.[11]

The term *sacrament* is not found in the New Testament. It is of Latin origin (*sacramentum*). Jerome used the term to translate the Greek term meaning "mystery" (*mystērion*) in the Latin Vulgate. Then in the early church, Tertullian identified baptism as a Christian sacramentum, indicating the early church interpreted the sacraments politically.[12] They were oath-taking pledges of loyalty to a new ruler.

Baptism as a Political Pledge

Baptism is a ritual signaling a political pledge. It functions as an insignia of allegiance to a new king. Jesus's followers would partake of a water sacrament to indicate their new citizenship.

Paul declares baptism as a political act. He says those who are baptized are baptized into Jesus's death and resurrection (Rom. 6:3–4; Col. 2:12; Gal. 3:27). But what do death and resurrection have to do with politics? In the Bible, resurrection was not only the

---

[8] Caesar, *Bellum civile,* 1.86.

[9] Livy, *Historiae,* 22.38.

[10] Tacitus, *Historiae,* 1.56.

[11] Quoted in Daniel G. Van Slyke, "*Sacramentum* in Ancient Non-Christian Authors," *Antiphon* 9, no. 2 (2005): 178.

[12] See R. Alan Streett, *Caesar and the Sacrament: Baptism: A Rite of Resistance* (Eugene, OR: Cascade Books, 2018), 2–4. I am dependent upon his work for this section. Tertullian, *De baptismo,* 4.4–5.

regeneration of an individual, but the restoration of a nation, even an army.

According to the Old Testament, resurrection was the rebirth of Israel's fighting residents and thus a sign of kingdom renewal. This can be seen in Ezekiel 37 and the story of the dry bones. Interpreters forget these prophecies are set after Nebuchadnezzar's invasion and destruction of Jerusalem. These bones are the slain Israelites defeated by Babylon. They lie massacred in a valley.

But God says that is not the end of the story. The prophecy about the dry bones is vivid imagery for the rising of Israel's army.[13] In the vision, Ezekiel is taken to a valley where he sees human bones. The bones are Jewish corpses whose flesh decayed and was eaten away. However, at the word of the Lord, a new spirit (breath) comes upon them, and they live! These dry bones grow new flesh, tendons, and sinew.

It's like in *The Lion, the Witch and the Wardrobe* when Aslan breathes on the statues, and they come back to life again to fight against the witch. Resurrection is the response to imperial oppression, as well as to death and sin. It is God's promise of a new society. In this way, resurrection hope is not only a personal and solitary event, but also a national, political, and communal event.

When Paul thinks of baptism, he connects it to resurrection. Baptism is the sign of God's new army. For example, Paul ties baptism to the crossing of the Red Sea in 1 Corinthians 10:2. As Israel *was* formed into a new political community, so the new Israel *is* *being* formed into a new political community. Baptism transferred

---

[13] See Streett, *Caesar and the Sacrament,* 65–72.

Israel from "in Pharaoh" to "in Moses." Today, baptism transfers people from "in sin, death, and in partisanship" to "in Christ."

Therefore, when we think of baptism, we should think of pledging loyalty to a new sovereign and forming a new political community. We die to our old allegiances and rise to new life. In baptism, we don our Sovereign's jersey and become his ambassadors.

The Lord's Supper and Resistance

If baptism is the political admission ticket, then the Lord's Supper is the continual rite of resistance. We typically think of the Lord's Supper as a formality at the end of services (and, too commonly, at the end of a service only every once in a while). In it, we get a stale piece of bread and cheap wine, or worse, grape juice. But this is nowhere near how the first-century church celebrated the Eucharist. It was a full-fledged meal that lasted hours. It was central to the worship service, not ancillary to it.[14]

Like all meals during this time, it had a social and political function. Meals preserve social values, regulate behavior, show honor to those we esteem, and transmit knowledge. The Roman meal was an instrument of social bonding and control. These were highly regulated banquets.

To attend, one had to be invited. Seating was structured according to status. Slaves and women were generally not allowed at the main table. Most of these meals enforced social boundary markers: elites ate with elites while peasants ate with peasants.

---

[14] In this section, I am indebted to R. Alan Streett, *Subversive Meals: An Analysis of the Lord's Supper under Roman Domination during the First Century* (Cambridge: James Clarke & Co., 2016), 31.

There were two different types of meals. Suppers were short-ened forms, but the expanded form of the meal included both the supper (*deipnon*) and the symposium (*symposion*). The symposium was an extension of the meal where people would drink and engage in discussion, entertainment, lecture, or other forms of social bond-ing and entertainment.

Joining these two segments of the banquet was the central action: the libation. The libation was when a cup of mixed wine was lifted and poured out. The host or *symposiarch* (leader of the feast) would lift the cup in honor of the emperor or some deity and pronounce a blessing. They would then pass this cup around. Everyone would drink from it, affirming the benevolence of their divine host.

These meals were political rituals, honoring the emperor. There is some research to indicate Rome imposed two obligations upon these associations. First, they must honor the emperor with a liba-tion at the meal. Second, they could not participate in any political action against the state.[15]

This lens informs our perception of the Lord's Supper. When Jesus conducted this meal with his disciples, he subverted certain tropes associated with these banquets. Paul says after they broke bread, Jesus took the cup and interpreted it as his blood (1 Cor. 11:25; cf. Matt. 26:27; Mark 14:23; Luke 22:20). Jesus was act-ing as the *symposiarch,* transitioning from the meal to the sympo-sium. But instead of honoring a deity or the emperor, he blessed the Father, and pointed to the wine and bread as a symbol for himself.

---

[15] Streett, *Subversive Meals*, 46.

Paul says when the church drinks the cup and eats the bread, they proclaim the Lord's death until he comes. If they do so in an unworthy manner, they sin against their King (1 Cor. 11:26–27). Rather than following the social and political ideology of the day, Christians were pledging their loyalty to another king at the Lord's Supper.

You might be thinking, wasn't the Lord's Supper related more to the Passover than to Roman suppers? But even the Jewish background also indicates the political nature of this meal! Hebrew slaves prepared the Passover meal under the weight of Egypt's oppression. They ate the meal in anticipation of God's liberation.

On the night of the Passover, God supernaturally destroyed all the firstborn in Egypt by the angel of death. The firstborn of Pharaoh would have been the next king. God thus strikes at the heart of the regime by cutting down its next ruler. But he preserves the firstborn in Israel, indicating he will be their king. The food, drink, stories, and songs would transport them back in time to Egypt, where God had delivered them from their enemies.

When both of these backdrops are fused into our view of the Lord's Supper, it becomes clear the meal is much more than a formality devoid of any political meaning. The meal reminds the church that God provides a new way for his firstborn people. A new exodus. A new redemption. This is not only a "spiritual or symbolic" meal, but one bursting with political meaning. It declares and reenacts our liberation.

Conclusion

We all practice our faith in political contexts. As we saw at the beginning of this chapter, Bonhoeffer practiced his subversive faith in the most radical way. But Bonhoeffer was not alone. Karl Barth also lived at the same time.

He was born in Switzerland in 1886 and became a well-known Christian professor. He found himself lecturing in Germany when Hitler rose to power.

Opinions about Hitler divided the German church. The majority of Christians supported Hitler's war, but Barth was critical of Hitler. He was largely responsible for writing *The Barmen Declaration*, which rejected the influence of Nazism on German Christianity.

Barth argued that the church's allegiance belongs to Jesus Christ. He personally mailed the declaration to Hitler. In 1935, Barth was forced to resign his professorship at the University of Bonn for refusing to swear an oath to Hitler. Here's one of the oaths he declined:

> I swear by God this sacred oath, that I will render unconditional obedience to Adolf Hitler, the Führer of the German Reich and people, Supreme Commander of the Armed Forces, and will be ready as a brave soldier to risk my life at any time for this oath.

Barth was tried for insubordination and found guilty. He recognized the Christian message is deeply political. Both Jesus and Paul proclaimed messages of political subversion. For Barth, this meant standing up to Hitler and his regime. He could not render "unconditional obedience" to anyone but his Lord Jesus.

Christianity does not merely have implications for the public square. It is itself a politic. Christianity is another way. It subverts any other regime that claims to provide peace, security, freedom, and happiness.

However, questions still linger about the nature of this subversion. Questions like: *Were the accusations against Paul true? Why was he consistently declared innocent? If the church is a political assembly, then why do baptism and the Lord's Supper seem like innocent rituals?*

We will explore these in the next chapter as we combine the way of subversion with the way of submission.

CHAPTER 5

The Way of Submission

Appealing to Caesar

The 2019 film *A Hidden Life* tells the story of Franz and Jani Jägerstätter. They are Austrian peasant farmers in World War II. Much of the movie is set in the beautiful mountains of Austria. The camera continually pans across the fields and hills, showcasing Franz and Jani's love for their scenic home.

Franz is devoted to his country, but he decides he will never swear an oath to Hitler or fight for him. When he refuses to "Heil Hitler," he is arrested as a traitor. But this protest actually shows his loyalty to true Austria. Franz's allegiance to his homeland stands above this false ruler.

When Franz is in prison, he writes a letter to his wife saying, "Oh, my wife. What's happened to our country? To the land we love?" Franz is caught between loyalties, but he understands one loyalty trumps all others.

Like Franz, the church needs to decide which allegiance is paramount. This means, like in Franz's case, both submitting and subverting coming together. Franz refused to fight or pledge loyalty to Hitler, but he willingly submitted to the state's punishment.

In the same way, the church's stance toward the state combines both subversion and submission. To use the language of Kavin Rowe, Christians say: "New culture, yes—coup, no."[1]

We have seen how Paul *entered* the courtroom, but we also must examine how he *exited*. We have seen how the church is a political assembly. Now we must examine her policies. We have seen how baptism and the Lord's Supper are rites of resistance, but we must look to *what* they teach us to resist.

The kingdom's values do not mesh with the world, but Jesus's followers are not against Rome *as Rome*.

Paul's Innocence

Paul disrupted economies, subverted the Empire, and was accused of going against Roman law. However, the great irony is that Paul was also *declared innocent* by the governing authorities. The charges were dismissed.

The trials in Acts have a beginning and an end. There are accusations and acquittals. We can't speak about one without looking at the other.

At the end of Acts, Paul comes before numerous Roman judges (Acts 24–28). As detailed in the last chapter, Paul is accused of

---

[1] C. Kavin Rowe, *World Upside Down: Reading Acts in the Graeco-Roman Age* (Oxford University Press, 2010), 5.

being an agitator, a plague, a leader of a rebellion, and someone who desecrated the temple (Acts 24:5–6). But Paul denies these charges.

He says, "Neither against the Jewish law, nor against the temple, nor against Caesar have I sinned in any way" (Acts 25:8). Paul asserts he is innocent of any political insurrection. He is not the leader of a rebellion, and his aim is not mutiny. His ministry has been pure, undefiled, and virtuous.

Surprisingly, Paul's judges agree. Claudius Lysias, the Roman officer who rescues and almost beats Paul, says the accusations against Paul concern Jewish law, and no charge merited death or imprisonment (Acts 23:29). Festus says Paul hasn't committed the evils he had expected. Agrippa talks with other rulers, and they conclude Paul has done nothing to deserve death or imprisonment (26:31).

Paul then drops a bomb on the most extreme forms of subversion: he climactically appeals to Caesar (25:11). The apostle is so confident in his innocence that he is willing to stand before Caesar. If Paul's message is anti-government, then this request makes little sense. His kingdom is of another world.

Paul is confident that he has done nothing against the state. Our tendency, if we don't like the way our authorities are directing us, is to hit the gas pedal on subversion. But if we like the way it is going, we speak of how Paul entrusted himself to the governing authorities. Paul shows these realities must lie in tension.

Paul viewed the Christian message as subversive but also virtuous, innocent, and submissive. Christ's kingdom was still to come, but also present. In this way, the charges against him were both true and false. His proclamation of King Jesus promoted a new way of life, a new kingdom. But this life could exist amicably in the Roman Empire. Paul was innocent enough to stand in front of the opposing king.

Paul aimed never to break the law or to cause unnecessary agitation. Though his message did agitate, the offense was not in Paul's actions. Even so, Paul viewed both his message and his actions as above reproach. He had confidence that, if tried fairly, he would leave the courtroom exonerated.

A Dual Citizen in Philippi

Paul was not only innocent in court. In Philippi Paul shows he is a dual citizen, both of the kingdom of God and of Rome (Acts 15:36–16:40).

In Philippi Paul is accused of disturbing the city, promoting customs not legal for Romans to practice. Then he is stripped, beaten, and thrown into jail (Acts 16:20–22). Yet in all this, Paul displays he is not only innocent of seeking to harm Rome, but actually works for Rome's well-being.

After a divine earthquake sets Paul and Silas free from prison, Paul views it not as an opportunity for freedom, but an opportunity for service and proclamation. His liberation would have come at the expense of the jailer's life, but the jailer is not Paul's enemy. The open jail doors provide an open door for the gospel. They provide a path to share Jesus's life-giving presence with a soldier who would be under Caesar's death sentence.

Paul calls out to the jailer, telling him they are still there (16:27–28). The jailer recognizes the virtue of these prisoners and asks them what he should do to be saved. Luke juxtaposes life and death in this narrative. God, through Jesus, offers life. The jailer's commanders require death. The jailer has his eyes opened to a more benevolent ruler.

Paul welcomes this guard into the family and army of God, showing that he is not against those who work for the state. He reaches out even to those who imprison him and welcomes him into the kingdom.

Paul is primarily a citizen of the kingdom above, but that does not mean he is against the state below. The jailer and Paul, the prison guard and the prisoner, share a meal together in a home.

Paul not only welcomes the jailer, but he announces his own Roman citizenship (16:38–39). In a Roman colony, Paul exuberantly proclaims a new reign *and* happily remains a citizen of Rome.

Like all Christians, Paul was a dual citizen. He was a citizen of the kingdom of heaven, but also an earthly citizen. These two are not necessarily at odds. Paul shows this is the case for all Christians by acknowledging their dual identities.

- He writes to those *in* Rome, but loved *by* God (Rom. 1:7).
- He writes to the church *at* Corinth, those sanctified *in* Jesus Christ (1 Cor 1:2).
- He writes to those both *at* Ephesus, and faithful *in* Christ (Eph. 1:1).
- He writes to the saints who are *in* Philippi, and *in* Christ (Phil. 1:1).
- He writes to the saints living *at* Colossae, and *in* Christ (Col. 1:2).

The "double address" in Paul's letters is crucial. We have dual citizenship. We can submit to the state and to God. But our primary identity is in Christ. Paul came to Philippi to proclaim the reign of a new king, a new society, but that did not revoke his Roman citizenship.

Paul longed for a new city whose foundation is built by God. Still, his place on earth compelled him to seek the good of those on earth by telling them of the coming kingdom. He recognized the state would never salute him for his service. Instead, they would arrest him, beat him, and kick him out of town. They didn't have the categories to understand how his ultimate allegiance to Jesus compelled him to submit to the state.

I write these words while in Cannon Beach, Oregon, on January 6, 2021. I keep trying to work on this book, but the news cycle has me distracted. I can't keep my eyes off the updates. Some supporters of Donald Trump took over the Capitol of the United States and shut down a congressional assembly.

This came after a year that included many downtown riots in major cities across America. Far-left groups like Antifa and others took over the streets, looted stores, and spray-painted downtown businesses—which I saw firsthand living in Portland. While not all of the gatherings had this aim, some sought to overturn the social order through violence, pillaging, and ransacking.

As I mentioned earlier, throughout the process of writing this book and sharing its argument with friends, many have questioned me on whether the term "subvert" is the right one to use. It is natural to wonder, today of all days, and this year of all years, "Is this what subversion looks like?"

Does subverting the government mean storming the Capitol, refusing to wear masks, or rioting in the streets?

Does it mean seeking to overthrow the current regime? Working against the state? Blocking all their policies?

Does it mean destroying property, vandalizing buildings, setting things on fire?

As the above evidence shows, this is not how Paul advocated for the kingdom of God. Yes, Paul was arrested, beaten, thrown into prison, and accused of subverting the Empire. Yet, Paul did so in a way that did not implicate him in any wrongdoing. This is what the apostle Peter had in mind when he called Christians to endure the hardship they may experience for doing good, but also asked, "What credit is there if when you do *wrong* and are beaten, you endure it?" (1 Pet. 2:20, emphasis added).

In other words, there's nothing *Christian* about sinning against the government in our attempts to subvert it.

Any biblical notion of subversion must reckon with these verses. Any form of political discipleship must recognize Paul proclaimed a political message *and* was declared innocent in court.

Submitting to and Honoring Rulers

You might be surprised it has taken me this long to get to the most explicit commands for how we are to relate to governing authorities, found in Romans 13 and 1 Peter 2.[2] Both of them call Christians to submit to governing authorities. I waited to introduce

---

[2] See also Titus 3:1.

these passages purposefully. I wanted you to take a hard look at Jesus and Paul's lives before we examine the apostolic commandments.

I was compelled by another reason to hold off on these texts. Too often, political discipleship in some evangelical churches equals reading Romans 13 and 1 Peter 2 and closing the Bible. People act as if that is all the Scriptures have to say about the church's political formation. This is quite restricted and limited.

> **Too often, political discipleship in some evangelical churches equals reading Romans 13 and 1 Peter 2 and closing the Bible.**

Yet, while these passages aren't *all* the Bible has to say about Christian politics, they are critical texts in our political development. Overlooking them would be like skipping the Grand Canyon while driving through Arizona. Therefore, we must integrate Romans 13 and 1 Peter 2 into our political theology.

> Let everyone submit to the governing authorities, since there is no authority except from God, and the authorities that exist are instituted by God. So then, the one who resists the authority is opposing God's command, and those who oppose it will bring judgment on themselves. For rulers are not a terror to good conduct, but to bad. Do you want to be unafraid of the one in authority? Do what is good, and you will have its approval. For it is God's servant for your good. But if you do wrong,

be afraid, because it does not carry the sword for no reason. For it is God's servant, an avenger that brings wrath on the one who does wrong. Therefore, you must submit, not only because of wrath but also because of your conscience. And for this reason you pay taxes, since the authorities are God's servants, continually attending to these tasks. Pay your obligations to everyone: taxes to those you owe taxes, tolls to those you owe tolls, respect to those you owe respect, and honor to those you owe honor. (Rom. 13:1–7)

Submit to every human authority because of the Lord, whether to the emperor as the supreme authority or to governors as those sent out by him to punish those who do what is evil and to praise those who do what is good. For it is God's will that you silence the ignorance of foolish people by doing good. Submit as free people, not using your freedom as a cover-up for evil, but as God's slaves. Honor everyone. Love the brothers and sisters. Fear God. Honor the emperor. (1 Pet. 2:13–17)

Submission to Governing Authorities

At surface level, Romans 13 seems easy to understand. The most common view is to take the text at face value. Paul argues for submission to the government for three reasons. *First, governing authorities have been appointed by God* (13:1b). Those who oppose these rulers oppose God, since he has installed them. If you disobey earthly authorities, you disobey God.

Second, rulers are servants of God who reward good behavior and punish evil behavior (Rom. 13:3–4). These rulers are placed in their positions to rightly order society, promote virtue, and establish public peace. If citizens disobey, there will be chaos and wrath for both them and the rest of humanity.

Third, Christians are to submit because of inward conscience (Rom. 13:5). Conscience is the inward capacity for moral judgment. Paul says people know God uses governing authorities as a part of his divine plan. God has ordered the world, and his ordering is good. Therefore, for the sake of our innate awareness of God's employment of governing authorities, we should submit.

The strength of this interpretation is clarity and straightforwardness. In many ways, Romans 13 can be seen as the "Achilles' heel" of subversive readings. The problem comes with the exceptions and questions that arise.

Paul unequivocally says people must be subject to governing authorities. It seems to be an uncompromising endorsement of political authority. But good questions arise, bringing doubt on whether this interpretation is as comprehensive as some suppose.

Does this text give license to tyrants, leading to horrendous abuses of power?

Does it square with moments in history like the American Revolution or the Civil Rights Movement?

How do we correlate this with other texts in the Scriptures, which associate pagan governing authorities with Satan?

Does this command urge an unthinking approval of everything governing authorities do?

Jettisoning the clear command to submit because of the difficulties seems to go against the plain meaning of the text. Explaining it away might encourage insurrection. But an unquestioning call to submit at all times doesn't seem consistent with other parts of Scripture, like those we've already considered. So, what are we to do with this text?

Some interpreters have begun to emphasize other aspects of the text. They interpret the commands with the larger literary context. Paul applies the principle of pursuing peace and harmony in Romans 12:9–21 and therefore instructs them not to rise up like in warfare like ancient Israel. They also point to the historical context, saying that Paul says to submit because they needed to protect a vulnerable community against ruthless rulers.

These contexts could constrain Romans 13 as specific to the culture of the time. Paul instructs Roman Christians based on *their* particular circumstance. Romans 13, in this view, cannot be wielded as a full-blown political theology.

Both the plain and the contextual reading of the text have their strengths and weaknesses. I lean toward a plain reading, with some nuances. The problem with both views is when they are applied with a heavy-handed approach. The outworking of the first view might say this is our *only* response to governing authorities. In contrast, the implications of the second view say this was *only* for that particular context, and has no relevance for us today. We need a more balanced view.

Paul is not legislating every situation in Romans 13, nor is he addressing every condition. He doesn't distinguish what to do with tyrants, when it is appropriate to rebel, or when governments have forsaken their authority. That's not his aim in the text. But he is giving the *standard posture* we should have toward rulers.

You might think, "Wait, Paul doesn't know the type of rulers we live under." But remember, Rome was no "city on a hill" promoting justice and the welfare of its citizens. Their emperors were far more corrupt than our rulers. And still, Paul commands submission. This means our knee-jerk reaction to the government should be deference, respect, and obedience. It means our "rugged individualism" needs a good dose of "keep calm and carry on." Negative responses to the government should be the exception, not the norm.

We might be tempted to evade our civic duties under God's reign, but Paul says, "Hold the phone." Because God has installed these rulers, we are to submit to them.

Honoring the Emperor

Peter gives similar commands in 1 Peter 2:13–17. We know Peter writes to a suffering community, but we don't know if it was suffering at the hands of the government. Yet, in the midst of their suffering, Peter affirms both the sovereignty of God *and* the genuine authority of the state.

He tells those in Asia Minor to be subject, to submit themselves to every human authority. Like Paul, Peter affirms that loyalty to Christ does not equal rebellion. Peter says we are to submit. Not merely to some authorities, but to every human authority. He writes about both lower and higher rulers: emperors and governors.

The reason to submit to them is the same as in Romans. First, because Jesus put them in their place of rule (2:13). Second, because rulers punish what is evil and praise what is good (2:14).

Unique to Peter is the final reason for submission: witness. By submitting, we will silence foolish people who might accuse us of disorder. Peter says opponents should have nothing to pin on us. We should be upstanding citizens for the sake of evangelism.

Did you hear that? How you respond to the government is part of your witness. This is not an issue Christians can agree to disagree about. It is part of how we witness to the world about the reign of Jesus.

Yet, even amid arguing for submission, Peter humbles these rulers with a few key moves. First, Peter says they are "human" or "created" authorities (2:13). Against the emperor-worshipping cult, Peter says these rulers are merely creatures. They are not the supreme authority. They are created beings who will die like the rest of humanity.

Second, we are to submit as *free people* (2:16). Ultimately, God is our authority, but his authority compels our submission. Only free people can genuinely submit. Submission is an expression of freedom. We are God's slaves, and therefore free from all other rulers.

> Only free people can genuinely submit. Submission is an expression of freedom.

Ironically, this freedom compels submission. Freedom is not self-determination, but service. Not self-fulfillment, but self-emptying.

Third, Peter gives a summative statement. In many ways, the entire thesis of this book is contained in 1 Peter 2:17.

> Honor everyone.
>> Love the brothers and sisters.
>> Fear God.
> Honor the emperor.

I purposely placed the text in an A-B-B-A format so you could see the parallels. We are to honor the emperor, but also honor everyone (2:17). In a time where the emperor required the most honor, Peter levels the distinction and says to honor all people like you honor the emperor. Submission and subversion. With a few words, Peter has flattened the status pyramid of the Roman Empire. He has said the treatment of a slave should be the same as the treatment of the emperor.[3]

Centrally, they are to love the brothers and sisters and fear God (2:17). Peter reserves the word "fear" for God and "love" for the brotherhood. Those in Asia Minor are dual citizens. They are to honor all (even the emperor) but reserve a special place in their hearts for God and his people. They have dual loyalties. But these loyalties don't always have to compete. There is an order.

Peter, like Paul, commands honor and submission to governing authorities. He says we should do so as part of our witness to the world. This is what we saw in Paul's life. This is what we saw in Jesus's life. And if a servant is not above his master, we must follow in the steps of Jesus, not forging our own path but following the one already trodden by him who has gone before us.

---

[3] This language is dependent upon Joel B. Green, *1 Peter*, The Two Horizons New Testament Commentary (Grand Rapids: Eerdmans, 2007), 76.

The Suffering and Inclusive Church

The church is a political assembly—an outpost of the kingdom advocating for her ruler's will. However, while we have a political charter, our sovereign is hidden. He is to be discerned by faith. His kingdom marches forward by a politic of persuasion rather than force.[4]

Therefore, specific actions mark this political community. You might expect the church to take up arms or attempt a coup-de-tat as it advocates for a new kingdom. But this is not how we march into battle.

Peter's first letter shows us how the church is an exile and sojourner on earth. Though a sojourner in a foreign land, the church welcomes all to her new *polis* through both baptism and the Lord's Supper.

The Church and Her Exile Identity

In Asia Minor, the situation was dire. It was not as though the church was ignored, viewed positively, or unseen. It was at odds with the broader society. Christians didn't have peaceable relationships with their neighbors. They were viewed as a threat and an annoyance. The community was slandered (1 Pet. 2:12), endured grief (2:19), suffered unjustly (2:19; 3:14; 4:1, 19; 5:10), and was insulted (2:23).

How were they to respond? How are we to respond to cultural pressures? Are we to run and hide? Are we to rise and fight?

---

[4] Oliver O'Donovan, *The Desire of the Nations: Rediscovering the Roots of Political Theology* (Cambridge: Cambridge University Press, 2008), 166.

Peter reminds us we are exiles and sojourners (1:1, 17; 2:11; 5:13). Christians are passing through this land, but it is not our ultimate home. We wander like Abraham and Israel, waiting for the city from God.

In the meantime, we are not against the world but for it. We seek to bless the nations amid our sojourning. The exile assembly is given some surprising advice. As a body politic, we are to conduct ourselves honorably among the Gentiles (2:12).

We are to act virtuously, despite the antagonism. As visitors here on earth, we are to be good guests. Insofar as it relies upon us, we live quiet lives, avoid negative stereotypes, and seek to do good to all people. We are to live among our neighbors (not separate from them), but in an upright way (avoiding evil). It is lifestyle evangelism.

Peter says if the Christian community is punished for doing evil, then that is no credit to us (2:20). But if we do good and suffer, then we are truly living as exiles. This is how light meets darkness. If we suffer because of righteousness, we are blessed (3:14). We are to suffer for doing good (3:17), not as a murderer, thief, evildoer, or meddler (4:15).

The actions of Christ's army are shocking. As Jesus said, his kingdom was not of this world, or his followers would take up the sword. Peter builds on this, saying to the baptized community that their weapons are love, peace, kindness, and goodness. The resistance they are to employ is non-violence, and they are to seek the good of others.

If you believe subversion means murder, stealing, meddling in other people's business, or doing evil, you have it all wrong. Subversion is neither storming the Capitol nor seeking to burn down Planned Parenthood centers. To subvert is to suffer and do good in response. We are dual citizens.

The epistle to Diognetus, a letter from a Christian apologist in the mid second century, describes our dual identity well.

> Christians are not distinguished from the rest of humanity by country, language, or custom. For nowhere do they live in cities of their own, nor do they speak some unusual dialect, nor do they practice an eccentric way of life. . . .
>
> They live in their own countries, but only as sojourners; they participate in everything as citizens, and endure everything as foreigners. Every foreign country is their fatherland, and every fatherland is foreign. They marry like everyone else, and have children, but they do not destroy their offspring. They share their food but not their wives. They are in the flesh, but they do not live according to the flesh.
>
> They pass their days on earth, but they are citizens of heaven. They obey the established laws; indeed in their private lives they transcend the laws. They love everyone, and by everyone they are persecuted. They are poor, yet they make many rich; they are in need of everything, yet they abound in everything. They are dishonored, yet they are glorified in their dishonor; they are slandered, yet they are vindicated.

> They are cursed, yet they bless; they are
> insulted yet they offer respect. When they do
> good, they are punished as evildoers; when they
> are punished, they rejoice as though brought to
> life.[5]

The basis of this peaceful presence is Jesus himself (2:21–25). Christ is the ultimate sufferer, the ultimate slave, the ultimate sojourner. He is our pattern, the outline around which we trace our behavior to. Though his death on the cross marked him as a rebel, it was actually his enthronement.

The church is a political assembly, but that does not mean we are to overthrow the government. We submit to it. It does not mean lashing out at those who persecute us but doing good to our enemies. We entrust ourselves to God. We live as exiles who long for a better country. We fight darkness with light.

Baptism and Inclusion

The church is a sojourning community, but one that welcomes new citizens and grows as it sojourns. Nowhere is the inclusive nature of the church seen more than in her sacraments. Though baptism is a sign of God's new army (a rite of resistance, and therefore subversive), the way baptism works surprises.

Baptism breaks down economic and ethnic barriers rather than preserving them. Most political communities use borders to define

---

[5] "The Epistle to Diognetus" 5:1–2, 5–16 in *The Apostolic Fathers: Greek Texts and English Translations,* 3rd edition, edited and translated by Michael W. Holmes (Grand Rapids: Baker Academic 2007), 701–2. I adapted the translation at places.

themselves, but we use water to wash away otherness. This rite of resistance doesn't *exclude* others but *invites* them.

From the Old Testament, it might seem that Israel would be restored and then go on to conquer the other nations with the sword. And they do conquer, but they only do so through the Spirit of peace. The same rebirth they have experienced is offered to all nations in Acts.

- Samaritans, who are nontraditional mixed-race Jews, are baptized (Acts 8:12).
- A eunuch, one aligned with another kingdom, is welcomed (8:36).
- Saul, an enemy of the church, is included (9:17–19).
- A centurion, someone who serves Caesar in Caesarea, is baptized (10:47–48).
- Two households in Philippi, a rich woman named Lydia, and the jailer, go under the water (16:15, 33).
- Crispus, the leader of the Jewish synagogue in Corinth, is integrated (18:8).

The rite the apostles advocate is not one of opposition, but one of welcome. Here again, readers find an unnatural pairing. Outsiders are invited in, not trampled. They are welcomed, not rebuffed. They are included, not cast out. They exist under a new allegiance and still serve Caesar.

Therefore, the Spirit of baptism is not only a rite of resistance but also power for peace. Read Paul's words to the Corinthians under the banner of politics: "For we were all baptized by one Spirit

into one body—whether Jews or Greeks, whether slaves or free—
and we were all given one Spirit to drink" (1 Cor. 12:13). The
Spirit forms a new body politic.

> For through faith you are all sons of God in Christ
> Jesus. For those of you who were baptized into
> Christ have been clothed with Christ. There is no
> Jew or Greek, slave or free, male and female; since
> you are all one in Christ Jesus. And if you belong
> to Christ, then you are Abraham's seed, heirs
> according to the promise. (Gal. 3:26–29)

The social, ethnic, and economic distinctions were washed
away with baptism. It was a rite of resistance, but one in which
harmony and love were the weapons of warfare.

The Lord's Supper and Inclusion

We have seen how the Lord's Supper resembled Roman banquets. In this way, it was a rite of resistance where Jews would
honor Jesus Christ as their benefactor instead of Caesar. The new
Israel would remember the liberation from Egypt, their liberation
in Christ, and the final liberation to come. However, the innocent
nature of this meal again surprises.

To attend Roman banquets, one had to be invited by the host.
While there, certain rules applied. Only free men could recline at
the table. Slaves were not allowed at the table at all, and if a woman
attended a banquet, she sat beside her husband's couch. Women
rarely attended the symposium portion of the meal.

The banquet was designed to solidify lower and higher class structures. Peasants would feast with peasants while the elite would recline with the elite. Even banquet seating was carefully arranged to identify one's status.

Jesus and the church defied these traditions. They saw the table as a sacrament where those baptized would share their goods, no matter what their social status. In Luke, Jesus employs the table as a vehicle to promote God's social values for the kingdom. He ate with sinners and outcasts, women, children, slaves, and even those who worked for Rome. Jesus "raises the poor from the dust and lifts the needy from the ash heap, to make them sit with princes, with the princes of his people" (Ps. 113:7–8 ESV).

> Jesus employs the table as a vehicle to promote God's social values for the kingdom.

Jesus welcomed Levi and Zacchaeus, tax collectors who amassed wealth for Rome by robbing the Jewish people (Luke 5:27–39; 19:1–10). Although the Pharisees criticized Jesus for this activity, Jesus ate with them too (7:36–50; 11:37–54; 14:1–24).

Jesus employs the meal as an avenue to showcase his kingdom agenda. It was not a private meeting where they plotted against others. It was not a closed-off group where they stole from others. All who wanted to follow this king were welcomed to this meal. The true Symposiarch invited everyone.

Paul's teaching follows the tradition of Jesus. In 1 Corinthians, he commands that the table needs to be governed by an ethic of equality (11:17–34).

In Corinth, the wealthy Christians were not waiting for their poor brothers and sisters when they observed the Supper. They were eating before the others arrived, leaving very little for the poor. Their meals were more reflective of the Roman values of exclusion and hierarchy than the kingdom values of inclusion and equality.

Paul says this directly contradicts the meaning of the Supper. No VIP cards are needed around the table, only trust in the blood of Jesus. Communion was meant to showcase the unity of believers around their benefactor Jesus Christ. It should exhibit the harmony of the family of God. The Lord's Supper enacted a new social ethic.

The beating heart of the table is blood. It is a place to ponder and remember the liberation of God's people from Egypt. But Jesus reinterprets this as liberation from sin. The table is not a place where early Christians planned their liberation from Rome—or where we plan our liberation from whichever American political party we don't like. No, the table is a place where we remember how Jesus had liberated us from the power of sin and death.

At the Passover, God destroyed Pharaoh's firstborn to liberate his firstborn, Israel. At the Lord's Supper, Jesus told the disciples God would now sacrifice his firstborn. It was not the blood of their enemies which they remembered, but the blood of their king. The feast embodied Jesus's sacrificial politic.

Our meal declares Jesus's kingdom is not of this world. It celebrates the death of our innocent king, strung up on a Roman cross so that he might be exalted. It is a meal to celebrate the radical unity and equality of those Rome placed on separate levels of a rigid hierarchy. The Lord's Supper is both subversion and submission.

The Lord's Supper must continue to guide our political lives. It proclaims a politic of inclusion, equality, and peace. Communion engrains this identity into our bodies as we feed on the body and blood of our Savior.

Conclusion

In the last chapter, we looked at Karl Barth's critique of the German state. He lost his job because of his subversive stance. But I left out Barth's positivity toward the state, even when Hitler's atrocities made it easy to discount Germany. Barth argued the state is founded on divine providence, so the church cannot be against the state. She has to be for it, but also must transcend it.

The *Barmen Declaration* made clear statements about authorities of the state and the church. It spoke of the divine appointment of the state and how it has the task of maintaining justice and peace. The church must willingly acknowledge the benefit of the state. It also rejects that the church should take over the duty of the state.

Barth affirmed the distinct authorities of the church and the state. The state should not take on the vocation of the church, and the church should not take on the vocation of the state. They have separately defined functions. But this does not mean the church isn't a political entity. It simply has a different sphere of authority.

This chapter has countered a wrong view of subversion, but this does not contradict the reality of subversion.

Though Paul was accused of political insurrection, he was declared innocent.

Though the church is a political community, it submits to governing authorities and suffers for doing good.

Though baptism and the Lord's Supper are rites of resistance, their initiates resist by overturning social norms and welcoming all who will believe.

Therefore, the church's political posture is no different from that of Jesus. The way of subversion and the way of submission collide like the way of the kingdom and the way of the dove. This is the paradox of our political lives.

CHAPTER 6

Reimagining Politics with the Church

The Way of Submission and Subversion

I remember the night when Donald Trump was elected as president in November of 2016.

I stayed up late to watch the results, which is typical for me on election night. Hannah, my wife, was asleep on the couch. She took a snooze once she saw it was going to be a long process. She knows, better than I, that earthly rulers come and go.

At the time, we lived in Portland, Oregon. We had a neighbor who we had gotten to know. This neighbor was very excited about Hillary Clinton becoming the first female president. She had spoken to us for the past few weeks about how thrilled she was to see women progress in the country.

The night of the election, our neighbor dressed to a T. Pearls were draped around her neck, and she was in a formal dress anticipating the celebration. Like the rest of the world, she was stunned when Donald Trump won. Later that night, I found her stumbling up and down the street, drunk. Her makeup was smeared, and dark black lines streamed down her face from her tears.

We tried to comfort her, but to no avail. For many in Portland, it was clear their ultimate hope was in a certain party, a platform, a human savior. When that hope was not fulfilled, there was lamentation.

Christians are not immune to this. I heard a church in Portland had a "lament" service after the election in 2016 in an attempt to distance themselves from the religious right. Many politically conservative Christians, on the other hand, celebrated. Hope was alive again after eight long years.

These two responses reveal two of the political postures that allure us: *triumphalism* and *escapism*.

Triumphalism marries Christian hope and the state. It supposes a secular government has the power to usher in the kingdom of God. When "our" party succeeds, it is God's favor on the nation. This is an illegitimate marriage between the church and the state. When the church acquiesces to political power, her ecclesial power is eclipsed. She has sold her power, her keys, to the state.

Others of us reject this triumphalistic attitude but respond with escapism. We withdraw when things are not going right. God's judgment is on our country when decisions are made that are not in line with our view of "God's will." If the "other" side wins, it is time to detach. The church becomes a "besieged enclave" in a world gone to hell.[1] We cloister ourselves into our groups and let the state eat their just desserts.

---

[1] Lee Camp, *Scandalous Witness: A Little Political Manifesto for Christians* (Grand Rapids: Eerdmans, 2020), 123.

We get one of two mantras thrown at us, depending on which political party is in power. It is either "Withdraw, we're losing" or "Push forward, we're winning."[2]

Christians and Politics

Option 1 ——————— Faithfulness ——————— Option 2

Escapism ——————— Pilgrim ——————— Triumphalism

Neither of these postures represents the way the early church interacted with politics. They didn't view secular rulers as a Christian's triumph or defeat. That had already been decided on the cross. The question was how to act as citizens of heaven when they were currently citizens of earth.

Like Jesus, the early church has much to teach us about political formation in our current moment.

Governments Are Not the Enemy

In the last section, I argued Jesus affirmed governments as God's servants, and therefore, we need to honor them. I want to push this point even further. Paul and Peter argue governments are not only God's servants, but many times serve his good purposes.

Sometimes we get so frustrated by politics that we forget we have a vision for society that encompasses the state. Paul and Peter

---

[2] Jonathan Leeman, *How the Nations Rage: Rethinking Faith and Politics in a Divided Age* (Nashville: Thomas Nelson, 2018), 162–65.

explicitly say we submit to governments because God ordained them. But this raises the deeper question, why? At least two reasons exist.[3]

First, because God created all power for good. Power and authority can be corrupted, but in its proper use, it is virtuous. Governing authorities are good because they represent God's authority. God *mediates* his rule through these figures.

This might shock you. How could the governing authorities, with all their corruption and wickedness, be God's mediators? It's a good question and one worth pondering. Yet, the prophets affirm it about the great superpowers of Egypt, Assyria, Babylon, and Persia. Paul affirms it about those who will cut off his head. Peter does the same for those who will hang him upside down. And Jesus affirms it about those who string him up on the cross.

God created all power for good.

God employs non-Christian entities to bless the world, spread justice and peace, and allow gospel ends to be accomplished. Let me say this very clearly: *an institution does not have to be a "Christian" institution to do good.* God blesses the world consistently through non-Christian institutions. He does so through families, schools, and businesses. We should be the first to joyfully support such things for the benefit of humanity and the furtherance of the gospel.

---

[3] The following two points are dependent upon Lee C. Camp, *Scandalous Witness: A Little Political Manifesto for Christians* (Grand Rapids: Eerdmans, 2020), 112.

Therefore, even though governing authorities' power can be corrupted, we must affirm their rule. That is why Paul and Peter say these governing authorities exist to punish evil and reward the good. They are a tool for God to express his judgment and restrain evil. They preserve social order and justice so that the gospel might go forth.

Paul recognized this reality even while living in Rome. Rome could be both good and bad at the same time. It made roads that furthered gospel expansion, but also persecuted Christians and threw them in prison. Its laws protected citizens, but Rome was no friend of Christianity. Paul was willing to live in this tension. Christians need to follow his example.

This means we don't seek to overthrow the government (see the final section of this chapter for more on this topic). We don't engage in guerrilla warfare to fight the government. We don't stock up on ammunition to overthrow a regime. Christians submit to rulers because God has put them in place, and they exist for the good of humanity. Governing authorities are common grace.

Second, we recognize the government is not the real enemy. Christians are not anarchists! We, of all people, should be aware that defeating one political regime will not mean peace. The way to peace is not through mutiny, but only through the kingdom come. Tanks, guns, and ships can't defeat evil. Rome, Democrats, and Republicans are not the main enemy!

The fact that Jesus and Paul rarely criticized Rome directly displays their theological understanding of power. It was not a move away from politics but a deeper understanding of it. When they attacked the source of power, the demonic forces and our own flesh, they displayed that the empowerment of the new creation people was more important than the disempowerment of Rome. Freedom from Rome would not mean freedom for Israel.[4]

In the same way, freedom from the left or right won't mean liberty for us. Our sin problem runs much deeper than the man or woman up top, much deeper than a donkey or elephant. Until death is defeated and the kingdom has come, there are no utopian states, no perfect places, no ideal dwellings, no ultimate destinies. The final stage of history will not come through our rebellion or our party's election, but in Christ's return.

Therefore, we can press toward being a presence of peace while being realistic about ongoing sin and corruption. The city of man will *both* spread corruption and curb it. But its government is still legitimate and good because *a* government is better than *no* government. Order is better than anarchy.

> **Until death is defeated and the kingdom has come, there are no utopian states.**

Governing officials have been *ordained to promote order, stability, virtue, and justice.* These are political goods. Unfortunately, we tend to ride our bikes in two gears: perfect order or absolute chaos. We need to be able to ride at different speeds. Of course, secular governing authorities promote policies antithetical to the fullness of Christian faith and practice. But this does not mean the government is not still a good that should be celebrated and valued.

---

[4] Oliver O'Donovan, *The Desire of the Nations: Rediscovering the Roots of Political Theology* (Cambridge: Cambridge University Press, 2008), 95.

Therefore, throwing mud at one party is not our goal. A long line of "dark powers" is waiting, ready to take the throne once it is vacated. We recognize that no matter which party we associate with, there are dark recesses to both.

The primary task of our communities is not to run to secular political orders for protection, to dominate political processes, or to bring about the "Christian" state. The primary task is to stand as a witness to an alternative political society.

We must reject both power and passivity, both retaliation and retreat. There is a third way. Peter and Paul say submit. Appreciate the common grace while it lasts. Lean in for the good of humanity and the honor of God.

Dual Citizens

Not only are we called to recognize that governments are not the enemy, but we must also realize that as Christians, we exist as dual citizens. One citizenship does not cancel out the other, though one is primary. As Augustine argued, we live in the city of man and the city of God. Two political entities exist at the same time. These are interconnected, but not identical.

Paul affirms his dual identities. He is not afraid to claim he is a Roman citizen *and* an ambassador of the kingdom (Acts 16:37; 22:25, 27). The communities he writes to who reside *in Ephesus, Corinth, or Rome* are faithful *in Jesus Christ*.

The danger for Americans is either they will completely wed or divorce these citizenships. Merging these citizenships means believing that America (or any other nation) is God's chosen nation, the only hope for the world, and placing one's hope in political processes and elections. It is common to hear that America is a Christian nation. But this can't be true. No nation-state can be a Christian nation-state. This is not how Christianity works.

There are stark differences between Christianity and nation-states.[5] In terms of access, people enter Christianity by voluntary intention (faith and baptism), but usually enter nation-states by arbitrary historical accident (being born in the region).[6] Geographically, Christianity is transnational and bounded by no lines, but all nation-states are literally defined by borders.

Nation-states defend their borders by using military might and building walls, but Christianity has no interest in defending geographical borders. The gospel breaks down ethnic barriers and crosses borders to welcome all. In nation-states, the citizens are largely monocultural, but Christianity encourages diversity and multiformity.

Nation-states are interested in their own agendas, but Christians put others before themselves. To nation-states, their shortcomings are not living up to their ideals and potential, but Christians recognize their shortcomings stem from their corrupt nature. The hope of nation-states is utopia by their own ingenuity, but Christianity says utopia will only be brought by another.

---

[5] Camp, *Scandalous Witness*, 73–75. Some of the following comes from Lee Camp. I have added others.

[6] This point works for Baptists, not so much for Presbyterians. Sorry, not sorry.

The Difference Between Nation-States and Christianity		
Category	**Nation-States**	**Christianity**
Entrance	Arbitrary historical accident	Voluntary intention
Geography	Borders	Transnational
Defense	Army/military/building walls	Erases borders, breaks down walls
Citizens	Monochromatic	Multiform
Agenda	Their own interests	The interests of others
Shortcoming	Not living up to potential and ideals	Corrupt nature
Hope	In their own ingenuity	In the work of another

To claim that America is a Christian nation is a confusion of categories. America and Christianity are two very different things.

Some may insist this critique is too literal. What people mean by "a Christian nation" is a way of saying that our political traditions and values arose out of the Christian tradition. While this is partially true, look at what it has produced.

Churches fly American flags in their congregations. We celebrate July 4th with the same bravado as Easter. We endorse candidates. We invite presidents to speak at services or condemn the other party as the work of Satan or Jezebel. We combine the

> **To claim that America is a Christian nation is a confusion of categories.**

hope of the kingdom with the American dream. America becomes a city set on a hill that brings about kingdom ends.

The language of America as a Christian nation has done more harm than good, compelling us to sell our imperishable inheritance for a bowl of American stew.

With all of this swirling in our culture, some of us react to the marriage of Christianity and America by filing for divorce. Some of us see our citizenships as antithetical. We conclude that to be a kingdom citizen is to revoke our American citizenship. We refuse to identify with the earthly nation in which we reside. This is another error.

Paul viewed himself as both a Roman citizen and an apostle of Christ. These were not at odds. The reaction to Christian nationalism is often a rejection of our nation-state identities. We hear things like, "We're Christians, not Americans." When another president is elected, some will quip, "We have elected another Caesar." Or while explaining why Christians are completely detached from the world, "We are waiting for another kingdom."

This is the other extreme, not recognizing the complexity of our dual identities. There is a place for Christians to be patriotic. It is natural to have a certain affinity for that which is known, for what makes up the warp and woof of our lives. For a state, a city, a neighborhood, and even a country. We don't have to pit a general love against a more specific love.

For example, my parents are from Oregon, and I spent six years there. I have a certain connection to the geography and cultural distinctives. I have a unique love for Cannon Beach and the Columbia River Gorge and even the weirdness of Portland. You also become excited to get on a plane and return home, because those are your people and that is your place. In the same way, it is not wrong to have a love and respect for our country.

In *The Hiding Place*, Corrie Ten Boom tells the story of going to her nephew Peter's organ competition. This was two years after the fall of Holland to German occupation. Recently, an edict had made it a crime to sing the "Wilhelmus," the Dutch national anthem. Corrie and her family traveled to hear Peter play. At the end of the concert, Peter began playing the "Wilhelmus"!

> Father, at eighty-two, was the first one on his feet. Now everyone was standing. From somewhere in back of us a voice sang out the words. Another joined in, and another. Then we were all singing together, the full voice of Holland singing her forbidden anthem. We sang at the top of our lungs, sang our oneness, our hope, our love for Queen and country. On this anniversary of defeat it seemed almost for a moment that we were victors.[7]

To love our country or homeland is not a bad thing. This can become warped, but it would be warping a good thing.

An extreme of *divorcing* our dual citizenship produces a political relativism only possible for the privileged. If all we care about is the kingdom to come, then American policies to tear down systemic racism don't matter. Neither do rulings that help the homeless. Nor do policies that protect the unborn. If the earth is going

---

[7] Corrie Ten Boom, *The Hiding Place* (Grand Rapids: Chosen Books, org. 1971, updated 2006), 92.

to hell in a handbasket, then we can sit by and watch while we serve another king and kingdom.

The solution is to recognize distinction and overlap. There is a disparity between the kingdoms, but not comprehensive hostility. The church should follow in the tradition of Jeremiah by seeking the good of the city. But the church should not confuse the good of the earthly city with the city whose foundations were set in heaven.

> An extreme of *divorcing* our dual citizenship produces a political relativism only possible for the privileged.

Paradoxically, we should be the best citizens of the state because our citizenship is in heaven. But by "best citizens," I mean that we embody the Christian ideals of love, faithfulness, and service toward neighbors.

We have dual identities. They should neither be completely divorced nor completely married. However, as we will see in this next section, our citizenships are tiered. If you're reading this book, you're mostly likely an American, like me. But we have much more in common with our Nigerian or Korean or Australian brother or sister in Christ than our secular Republican or Democratic neighbor down the street. Our heavenly citizenship trumps our earthly citizenship.

Subverting the Empire

We have seen how we are to submit because rulers are mediators of God's authority. We have also pressed into our dual identities.

Yet whatever submission and dual citizenship does mean, it cannot mean "blind subjection." There are too many opposing biblical texts to consider. There are too many times people have, or should have, revolted against their authorities.

We have examples such as Paul who proclaimed a subversive message. Daniel, who defied the Babylonian Empire. Nathan, who critiqued and confronted Israel's king. John the Baptist, who spoke against King Herod's marriage. John the Apostle, who was exiled to the island of Patmos by Rome. And when the apostles were told to stop preaching the gospel, they said, "We must obey God rather than any human authority" (Acts 5:29 NLT).

What does all this add up to? We have *ordered* allegiances.

There is something Christians must yield to Caesar, but they must not yield what has previously been demanded by their Creator. Though Paul claimed he was a Roman citizen, he never sang, "I am proud to be a Roman, where at least I know I'm free" (as far as I know).

The million-dollar question is *when* and *how* do we subvert the state? No easy answers present themselves, but looking to the early church gives us some broad guidelines.

Be the Church

First, the church had minimal *direct* confrontation with the Empire. Though Paul's message was interpreted as defying Caesar, Paul did not denounce Caesar. He proclaimed another king; he didn't seek to unseat Caesar. His critiques were indirect and incidental, not direct or deliberate.

In the words of Oliver O'Donovan, a renowned Christian ethi-
cist who has made significant contributions to political theology,
"God has no spies; he has prophets."[8] The church speaks of God's
rule in prophecy and prayer, not through the gun and sword. The
Holy Spirit gives the church the authority to confront civil rulers.
The church prophecies to the world about Christ's reign and the
coming judgment. But she also prays for the world, asking God for
his mercy upon it (1 Tim. 2).

The church's subversion should take the form of a prophetic
word, not of an army or militia. A prophet speaks about the purpose and goal of history. We must be Elijahs to the Ahabs, Nathans
to the Davids, Nahums to Nineveh, Jeremiahs to Israel, and Pauls
to Caesar.

Paul did not view his audience with Roman governors or
Caesar as opportunities for power. He didn't think, "If I get in
good with them, then I can do so much more for the kingdom."
No. Ultimately his audience with the state was an opportunity to
preach the gospel. The fundamental way we can be politically subversive is by proclaiming God's kingdom and the gospel of hope,
forgiveness, and equality.

The church conquers and subverts the state from below, not
from above.[9] Paul wasn't interested in a top-down approach. The
church is a grassroots movement, as the kingdom is not a fully-
grown tree. It is a seed planted in the ground that grows slowly.
Sometimes this growth goes undetected because, in our new

---

[8] O'Donovan, *The Desire of the Nations*, 11, 187.

[9] O'Donovan, *The Desire of the Nations*, 193.

condition, we become better citizens of the state by reminding them of their duty.

The best way we can be politically subversive is not marching downtown, not seeking to install new judges who agree with us, not electing presidents who will promote Christian values—although all of these things might be limited goods. No, the best thing we can do is to establish strong political (not partisan) churches who proclaim the gospel of Christ that transcends any earthly party or politician. This is our primary political witness.

People long for communities where utopian ideals are proclaimed, even if not practiced perfectly. For the early church, to be politically subversive was to proclaim this message, baptize people, and celebrate the Lord's Supper.

> The fundamental way we can be politically subversive is by proclaiming God's kingdom and the gospel of hope, forgiveness, and equality.

We must be transformed before trying to transform society. We embody peace and justice in our communities before we have anything to offer the world. Therefore, Christians must first be involved in their churches, and must prioritize helping these communities be places that reflect the coming kingdom and its values of love, justice, righteousness, holiness, and equality. Above all, political witness will look like being part of and strengthening local assemblies.

Maybe that means we should stop watching so much cable news and get together with people in our congregations for meals, inviting others to do the same. Our political subversion is like a mustard seed. It may seem small, but this is the way of Christ's body. It will soon be a tree encompassing the earth.

Justified Subversion

However, we can't stop and simply say, "Be the church." More must be said. There is a place for us in the modern era to protest and even overthrow governments.

Two categories help us determine when reform, disobedience, and protest are justified. First, when the government has neglected, violated, or corrupted its role.[10] Second, when the government has extended its authority past its God-given role—what we could call infringement.

Two Categories for Justified Subversion		
Governmental Violation or Neglect	When the government has stopped ordering society, establishing justice (punishing the evil and rewarding the good), promoting virtue, and providing stability.	Reform
Governmental Infringement	When the government has stepped outside of its God-given jurisdiction. This could or could not involve sin, and we can question whether the commands have moral force over us.	Disobedience and/or Protest

[10] These categories overlap with some of the categories Jonathan Leeman gives in this article, "Must Churches Follow Mask Mandates?" 9Marks, September 20, 2021, https://www.9marks.org/article/must-churches-follow-mask-mandates/.

Responding to Government Infringement

Let's start with the second category—infringement—which has multiple applications, some of which are easier or harder to apply. There is a place for disobedience or protest when the government overextends its authority.

Only God possesses all authority. All other authority is relative and limited. It has boundaries. The government's authority extends to some spheres and not to others. As I have said, the government is tasked with promoting justice, order, virtue, and peace. For Christians, this means the government can't tell us who to baptize, how to conduct our worship, or what our doctrinal statements should say.

This is also the category to use when the government asks us to do something against what God has commanded. We should never obey their commands if they go against God's Word (Dan. 6; Acts 4:19–20; Rev. 14:6–13).

But this infringement category becomes more complex when the spheres of authority overlap. For example, God has given parents authority to raise their children, not the government. The Scripture says children are to obey their parents (Eph. 6:1).

However, the government should still punish parents who do evil to their children (abuse), or step in when parents are no longer fulfilling their responsibility. Raising children is both a private and public act. Therefore, both parents and the government have authority in this realm. The trick is figuring out where the line is.

Sexuality is another complex issue. The government, under natural law, can and should legislate some sexual norms. Incest, rape, and polygamy are rightly against the law. But the government must also recognize natural laws above them and therefore can't redefine gender or marriage. They can try, but this is not their prerogative. It is above their pay grade.

Another difficult example arose during the COVID pandemic. Local authorities said public gatherings had to cease for public health reasons. Some Christians argued this went beyond the government's authority because it applied to churches. Caesar shouldn't tell churches when they can meet. However, this was another case where there was overlap in authority. Churches have an obligation to meet, but the government also has an obligation to protect life.

As you can see, responding to governmental infringement is not a simple issue. We must be wise, learn from, and lean on each other to discern when subversion is justified.

Responding to Government Neglect or Violation

The second category for justified subversion is governmental neglect or violation. This is another way to say an unjust law is no law at all. Regimes whose policies are contrary to natural law, public order, and the natural rights of human beings have forfeited their authority.

In God's world, government follows a law that lies outside of it. Rules comes from God, and all humans know this law because of common grace. People know the difference between right and wrong because we are made in God's image.

When a government no longer rightly distinguishes the right from the wrong, when they perpetuate unjust laws, then protest, and maybe even overhaul, are justified. This is not because of our freedom as Americans but because of our freedom under God's rule. Exactly when and how this should occur is difficult to discern as the Scriptures don't give us clear guidelines on this, but a few things should be taken into consideration.

- First, one can't do this whenever you simply feel like it or dislike the government's direction. There must be good and convincing reasons for protest or overhaul.
- Second, the corruption must be widespread and all other options for reform must have been exhausted.
- Third, the level of the suffering of fellow-citizens should be measured.
- Fourth, non-violence should characterize the disobedience.
- Fifth, typically the protest and disobedience should be publicly disclosed to draw public awareness to the issue.

So for example, Christians could rebel against the American government in light of their unjust abortion laws. However, I don't think this fits all the categories above. There is still room for peaceful and law-based reform. All other options have not been exhausted. Christians can't rebel every time an unjust law is passed, but they can seek reform during corruption.

To give an opposite example, Dietrich Bonhoeffer, who was a convinced proponent of non-violence, concluded that it would be right to attempt to assassinate Adolf Hitler because all other options were closed to him. The widespread suffering of humanity that Hitler perpetrated made the move justified in his thinking.

This last example may cause us to think that we should just sit idly by unless another tyrannical ruler appears. In some traditions, we speak of civil disobedience only when we think something is in direct conflict against God's commands. But if we only protest when we are personally commanded to do something against God's will, it can grant license for us to ignore other injustices. Immigration, unjust warfare, murder of babies, sexual abuse, and racism come to mind.

We need to recover the idea of "mindful activism" for the good of our fellow brothers and sisters here on the earth when the government has neglected or corrupted its task.[11]

For example, it was *right* to fight against Jim Crow laws. It is *right* to protest against abortion policies. It is *right* to combat the porn-industry and sex slavery. It is *right* to advocate for policies that protect the earth and the family.

We can do these things because we recognize the decisions made by those in power sometimes need to be repudiated, discarded, or reformed. This is not a distinctly Christian move, but we should be especially compelled to participate because we believe in dignity, justice, and order for human society.

As Dietrich Bonhoeffer said: "Christianity stands or falls with its revolutionary protest against violence, arbitrariness, and pride of power, and with its plea for the weak. . . . Christendom adjusts itself far too easily to the worship of power."[12]

---

[11] Richard J. Mouw, *Politics and the Biblical Drama* (Grand Rapids: Eerdmans, 1976), 8.

[12] Dietrich Bonhoeffer, "My Strength Is Made Perfect in Weakness (Sermon for the Evening Worship Service on 2 Corinthians 12:9, London, 1934)," in

We don't protest because we believe our nation is the new Israel coming out of Egypt. Neither do we protest because we believe it will fix all our problems. We do so because we love our neighbors, seek their flourishing to the best of our abilities, and do so out of submission to our God.

At a local scale, this protest takes the form of capsizing pockets of injustice. We can all recognize times in history when seeking to overthrow aspects of a society was moral, and even imperative. In our system, this will be done largely through laws, since we are a law-based society.

For example, those Christians who knew about the redlining segregation policies in the 1930's New Deal should have fought them. The government sought to provide housing to white middle-class families in the suburban communities but left people of color out, pushing them toward urban housing projects.

The Federal Housing Association subsidized builders who were mass-producing subdivisions for white owners. But they required that no homes be sold to African Americans. This was a clear example of privileging one group over another. As citizens of another kingdom, Christians should have subverted these laws even if it meant losing favor among the elite.

Jagged and Straight Lines

Because of all the complexities, leaders should be slow to define the specifics of how individuals should destabilize. In the church,

---

The Collected Sermons of Dietrich Bonhoeffer, ed. Isabel Best (Minneapolis: Augsburg Fortress, 2012), 169.

we should recognize the difference between jagged and straight lines of application to moral injustices.[13]

A straight line is a moral issue that the Scriptures clearly address. For example, a church should denounce racism, abortion, and monetary injustice. These are straight moral lines that have ample biblical evidence.

The jagged line concerns *how* churches respond. Churches should speak against abortion, but it is another thing for churches to demand that their members stand outside abortion clinics and talk to people about it. This might be binding someone's conscience in terms of how they think the issue should be addressed. Churches should also denounce racism. But it is another thing to require members to address this problem by marching downtown.

Jonathan Leeman tells the story of Mark Dever, his former pastor in Washington, DC.[14] A US senator once invited Dever to his office for advice. The senator was a member of the church, and his was the last vote needed in the Senate to pass a constitutional amendment requiring a balanced federal budget—a major vote, no doubt. But he felt undecided.

He said to Dever, "My colleagues are pushing me. The party whip is pushing me. The press is hounding me. You're my pastor. How should I vote?"

Dever wisely responded, "Brother, I'll pray that God gives you wisdom."

---

[13] This concept is proposed by Robert Benne, but I have changed its meaning and application. Benne, *Good and Bad Ways to Think about Religion and Politics* (Grand Rapids: Eerdmans, 2010), 31–38.

[14] This entire story comes from Leeman, *How the Nations Rage*, 145–46.

Years later, recounting the story to Leeman, Dever told him, "It's not like I didn't have an opinion on the constitutional amendment. I had a very strong opinion."

Leeman said, "So why didn't you say something?"

"Because," Dever replied, "my authority as a pastor is tied to the Word of God. I know I'm right about the Bible. I know I'm right about the gospel and Jesus' promised return. And I'm happy to address any political issue that meets the criteria of being biblically significant and clear. Yet the constitutional amendment was neither biblically clear nor significant. Therefore, I am going to preserve my pastoral authority and credibility for the things that scripture has told me to talk about."

Dever went on to say if it had been something clearer in terms of biblical precedent, he would have had no hesitation in helping the senator out. While we may often agree on what the Bible says about a particular topic, we may not agree with what that means for public policy. Mark Dever didn't want to bind a person's conscience on this issue and say, "This is the Christian position" or even "This is how we must address it."

We know the Bible speaks about matters of public policy, but we cannot treat the Bible as a book of case laws.

Conclusion

When we moved to Kansas City in 2020, people would ask where we lived before moving here. I would say we moved from Portland, Oregon. During this time, downtown riots over racial injustice were on the nightly news. Many people looked at me and said, "It must be good to get out of that city and come to a more conservative state."

In one way, I knew what they meant. No one wants to live in a place where there is disorder, where businesses are being destroyed. Nobody wants to go to bed wondering what will happen at night.

At the same time, I found this odd. I wondered about the implication that Christians should flee places that see their political views as foreign. Paul did quite the opposite: he went straight for the cities where his views would be challenged.

Paul went into the hard cities. His message was not interpreted as a merely religious proclamation. Paul, like Jesus, was brought before the governing authorities and accused of subverting the state. Yet he still followed the way of submission. Paul was innocent before the state. He claimed he was not against Caesar, even appealing to Caesar for his innocence.

It is this same tension we must press into as we think about our political discipleship. We declare a message of a new King, but this message does not seek to unseat those who currently rule. In fact, because we recognize they are subordinate to God's good purposes for humanity, we submit to them and recognize they are there to do good. It is for this very same reason that we can subvert and protest.

PART 3

POLITICAL FUTURE

CHAPTER 7

The Way of the Lion

The Victory of the King

L oyalties compete.

Washington, like all other governing systems, pursues the devotion of its citizens. Walk into the US Capitol. Go to the rotunda and look up, and you'll see an example of how America tempts and trains us to view human authorities.

Above you is the *Apotheosis of Washington*. Painted in 1865, the circular form naturally draws your eyes to the center. There, you enter the heavens. In the middle is George Washington himself—highly exalted. His image is pictured above every other name.

Washington is dressed in purple and flanked by the goddesses Victoria and Liberty. In a circle around them are thirteen maidens, which represent the thirteen colonies. Across from Washington, a few maidens hold a banner with the phrase *E Pluribus Unum*, meaning "out of the many one." On the outer circle are six scenes representing war, science, maritime, commerce, mechanics, and agriculture.

The point is obvious. Washington's goal is to bring all these lowly, created things to divine use, thus bringing unity to the kingdom, and peace to all. From this painting, it is clear how people are to view American rulers. Leaders are to be revered. They are bringing forth the kingdom. They will bring lasting peace.

Washington has ascended and become a god (*apotheosis*), something the Roman people asserted about their rulers. We like to think we are different from Rome, but maybe not so much.

The end of the Bible (our political future) challenges us and warns us not to put too much trust in the city of man or give human governments undue recognition. Revelation shows the destruction of the city of man. It shows what will happen to those who worship what is temporary and passing. It addresses a significant number of Roman myths and counteracts them with the Christian message.[1]

We are also tempted to believe our empire will last forever to spread peace to the whole world, that wealth will increase forever, and that our national glories will know no end. We need only to elect the right leaders. But Revelation shows us every empire will fall. All empires will be footnotes of history. We can't place our hope in the city of man.[2]

---

[1] Michael J. Gorman, *Reading Revelation Responsibly: Uncivil Worship and Witness: Following the Lamb into the New Creation* (Eugene, OR: Cascade Books, 2010), 44.

[2] I borrow the following chart from Gorman, but I adapted it for my own purposes. Gorman, *Reading Revelation Responsibly*, 44.

Romans Myths	American Myths	Revelation's Subversive Counter-Myth
Empire	Nation-building	The Empire of Our God
The Roman Pax	Exceptionalism	Babylon, the Shedder of Blood
Victoria	Capitalism and Democracy	The Victory of the Lamb and His Followers
Faith (=loyalty to Caesar/Rome)	Allegiance	Keeping the Faith in Jesus
Eternity	Perpetuity	The Saints Will Reign with Christ Forever

In this chapter, we will look at the way of the lion. A lion conquers and destroys. Revelation and the Thessalonian epistles contrast two kings, two cities, and two returns. The city of man and the city of God cannot coexist forever, no matter what the bumper sticker says. One will endure forever; the other will be destroyed.

> The city of man and the city of God cannot coexist forever.

Reading Revelation Politically

I have always thought that the Disney movie *The Lion King* mirrors the biblical story. A future king is designated by an anointing and bright light, he is exiled from his home by one of his own family members, returns to conquer, shows grace, ultimately defeats death, ascends Pride Rock, and establishes the new creation.

Most importantly for our purpose is the reality that Simba returns to his homeland to claim the throne. It has been taken over by his uncle Scar, who has spread death and chaos. But Simba has a homecoming. He overthrows Scar and the hyenas and brings back healing to the land.

Revelation tells a similar story: the Lion King will return and all other kingdoms will fall. Revelation overflows with political imagery. Thrones, crowns, swords, and kings fill the scene as John paints his picture. The book of Revelation is essential for political discipleship.

But Revelation can either be underemphasized or overplayed in Christian circles. If overplayed, our political formation might become skewed toward rebellion and revolution. If underemphasized, our political theology becomes neutered.

We tend either to clasp onto Romans 13 (submit) when speaking of political theology or fasten onto Revelation 13 (subvert). Revelation 13 says the kings of the earth are sourced in Satan. We must take both Romans 13 and Revelation 13 together. It is a paradox.

The interpretation of Revelation is hotly debated so allow me to give three notes about how I approach the book.

First, *Revelation is not only about the future.* It also concerns the past and present. Like any good literature, it is first historically rooted, but it also transcends that historical moment. The first audience was the community in Asia Minor who struggled with Roman rule. John's first intention was to help them.

Revelation contains the clearest resistance literature. Worshipping the emperor in imperial cults was a temptation. Revelation shows that Christians were being required to participate in the imperial cult. Throughout the book, John gives hints of this situation, describing it as worshipping the beast or dragon (13:4–8; 14:9–11; 16:2; 20:4). As one New Testament scholar says, "The imperial cult was an elaborate 'God and country' phenomenon."[3]

However, John also expands his gaze and makes it applicable to all Christians. Significantly, the word "Rome" is absent in the book. This forbids us from limiting its meaning to the first century. In the words of another commentator, "Any society whom Babylon's cap fits must wear it."[4] Revelation is a critique of all state idolatries. Therefore, the last book of the canon speaks to every generation—past, present, and future—living under foreign governments who demand our loyalty.

Second, *Revelation is written in the form of an apocalypse.* John uses symbols and images to get his point across. This is important because Revelation peels back the layers to show what lurks below the calm surface of the waters. The literature does not conceal; it reveals.

In this sense, it has an illuminating and central function for our political theology. Revelation peers beneath the surface. When we see secular governments and wonder what stands behind them, John teaches us to look for the dragon, even when the dragon is not visible.

Third, *Revelation indicates the end has already begun.* The kingdom is already *and* not yet. That is why the book is for the past, present, and future—because we *all* live in the last days. The church is riding the wave of the future, but the future has not come fully yet.

---

[3] Gorman, *Reading Revelation Responsibly,* 41.
[4] Richard Bauckham, *The Theology of the Book of Revelation* (Cambridge: Cambridge University Press, 1993), 156.

Those in Asia Minor were already experiencing the birth pangs of the end. Already, the bricks in Babylon's wall were beginning to crack and tumble. It is appropriate to read backward from Revelation and apply the book to our modern age.

Therefore, Revelation has a revealing, regulatory, and illuminating function for our political lives. In many ways, the critique of the empire in Revelation is a critique of the church that participates in the myths the empire propounds. Will the church follow the Beast or the Lion?

The King of Kings vs. the Kings of the Earth

We are prone to think of Jesus as the King of our hearts, inward life, and soul. This is not how Revelation depicts Jesus. Following the Old Testament tradition, John affirms Jesus not only as the King of our hearts, but the King of kings. Like Simba, Jesus stands in opposition to all rulers who seek to govern the earth by darkness and death.

John begins describing Jesus as the "ruler of the kings of the earth" (Rev. 1:5). Jesus does not merely rule in heaven. His sovereignty extends over the planet. He is the Alpha and Omega, the beginning and the end (1:8). He has a long royal robe (authority), white hair (wisdom), and eyes like a flame of fire (judgment), and out of his mouth comes a two-edged sword (justice).

John enters the clouds of heaven and sees the true nature of his rule. At the center of Revelation, the center of the biblical story line, and the center of all of history, is the throne (Rev. 4–5). God's

throne stands above every earthly throne. Earth rulers are shadows
of the real thing. All of history pulsates from the heavenly throne.

John sees a scroll in the hand of the One on the throne. The
scroll represents redemptive history and God's purposes for creation. Only the Lion of the tribe of Judah, the Root of David, can
open the scroll. The Lion takes the scroll, showing he has authority
over the whole earth. The seals, trumpets, and bowls will issue forth
from this scroll. These are the King's judgments upon the earth and
the kings of the earth.

The Lion adjudicates, pours out his wrath, and conquers.
Salvation belongs to him. He commands an army of 144,000. The
characterization of the Lion is fiercely political. When this vision
is read against the backdrop of the Roman imperial cult, the Lion's
throne is supremely confrontational.

Opposing this Lion are the kings of the earth. They stand
against the King of kings, but they can't even challenge him. When
he opens the scroll, the kings of the earth, the great ones, the generals, the rich, and the powerful all hide themselves in caves among
the rocks of the mountains. They call out for the mountains to fall
on them, so they won't have to face the wrath of the Lion (6:15–16).

Who are the kings of the earth? The book has a few historical
hints connecting the kings of the earth to the Roman Empire. But
we also need to remember our first rule in interpreting Revelation:
it is about the past, present, and future. The kings of the earth
therefore are the kings of the earth! Surprisingly, pretty simple.

However, John makes it relevant to his own hearers, pointing to Rome in code. The first coded reference to Rome is found
in 2:12–13. The Lord Jesus says Satan's throne is at Pergamum.
Pergamum was the first province in Asia Minor to acclaim

Augustus Caesar. It became the center for the imperial cult. Jesus challenges the church to hold fast to his name and not deny their loyalty to the Lamb. Even Antipas was killed for being a faithful witness. Jesus stands opposed to the imperial cult.

The implication is clear. Jesus and emperor worship cannot coexist. Caesar's throne is Satan's throne. Only one throne rules over all. It can't get more subversive than this. Christians are being persecuted for not bowing to Caesar.

The second coded reference to Rome comes in Revelation 13:18. This passage contains the infamous mark of the beast. This beast arises out of the earth. He belongs to the dragon, and does signs and wonders. Through economic discrimination, people give their lives to him. The number of this beast is the number of man: 666.

Some think the mark of the beast is linked to Nero Caesar. Those in the first century tied numbers to letters and N-e-r-o-C-a-e-s-a-r can mean 666. The implication is that Caesar is the beast. The dragon animates him. John doesn't suppress his critique of the government.

Finally, Revelation refers to Rome in 17:9–11. John sees a beast with seven heads. Revelation 17 concerns the judgment of the great prostitute with whom the kings of the earth committed sexual immorality.

John then tells his readers the seven heads are seven mountains. There are seven kings, five of whom have fallen, one still is, the other has not yet come (17:9–10). Most see these seven as a reference to some combination of Roman rulers. John continues by stating Babylon will fall. Her city will be split into three parts, and she will drink the cup of God's wrath (16:19). Her city will become a desert, and she will be no more.

In summary, Jesus is characterized as the King of kings in Revelation—the Lion. The Roman Empire and her rulers, and thereby all kings of the earth throughout the eras, are set in opposition to God's Anointed One. They seek to mimic the sovereignty of God's kingdom, but the antichrist can only parody Christ's authority, as in *The Lion King*, where Scar is only a shadow of Simba's rule.

While Romans 13 teaches us God's kingdom and the kingdom of man can coexist temporarily, Revelation 13 stresses they cannot do so forever. The exiled King will return. There must be a winner. We already know the outcome.

Two Cities at War

If I were to ask Christians what the future of their city will look like, whether it be Boston, Kansas City, or Seattle, I am guessing not many would say it will be destroyed and replaced. But this is what we see in Revelation. A great replacement will occur, and the land will be cleansed.

The subversive nature of the last book of the canon is seen not only in the conflict between rulers, but in the opposition of their cities. Both sovereigns have followers, both kings have kingdoms, and both monarchies have metropolises.

Revelation presents two kinds of people. They are represented by two cities—Babylon and Jerusalem—and two women—a Harlot and a Bride. Only one will endure. The other will be shattered.

The name Babylon harkens from Israel's history and alludes to a nation that persecutes God's people. Babylon is connected to

Babel (Gen. 11:1–9). Babel was the first attempt to construct a city that opposed God. Human kingdoms are tempted to rival God's kingdom. Later Babylon is the city that brought Israel into exile (2 Kings 24–25). She worships her own culture and exalts herself. Babylon stands for any city that persecutes God's people and thus opposes God himself.

Peter and John employ the name Babylon for Rome (1 Pet. 5:13; Rev. 14:18; 17:5). John calls the woman the great city who has royal power over the kings of the earth (17:18). At first, she looks beautiful. She has scarlet clothes and jewelry. But in her cup is not wine, but the impurities of her prostitution. She has enriched herself by selling herself and persecuting those who won't bow to her. Babylon pours out the blood of God's people (16:6), and she drinks the blood of the saints (17:6; 18:24).

However, her end is assured. She will fall and become a desolate place. When this happens, every nation who has become inebriated off her, every king who has gone to bed with her, every merchant who has grown wealthy off her will weep and mourn because of her downfall. Babylon is the anti-city. She is opposed to God's rule and his people. This is not only true of Rome, but of all governments, past, present, and future.

Juxtaposed to Babylon is the New Jerusalem. She exists in the midst of Babylon, but climactically replaces Babylon in the end. After Babylon has been destroyed, the New Jerusalem comes down from heaven to earth prepared like a bride (21:2). Babylon looks like a pauper next to the radiance of New Jerusalem.

The New Jerusalem is made of precious stones. She has high walls and twelve gates. The city is a perfect cube, representing the Holy of Holies. She does not need a sun or moon because God's glory illumes her. Nations come to the city, kings of the earth bring their glory and riches to her. The gates of this city never close, and nothing unclean ever comes into it. In the middle is a river flowing from the throne of God and of the Lamb.

John intends to compare the two cities. That is clear, but so is the idea of replacement. The New Jerusalem displaces Babylon. The bride supplants the harlot. The kingdom of God sets its throne on top of Satan's kingdom.

The church will occupy the space the pagan empires covet. We should never be tempted to think our hope lies "elsewhere." Revelation says our hope is a throne from above that comes down and supplants the kingdoms of the earth.

Babylon vies for a future, but God's plan was always to have the New Jerusalem come from heaven. Worldly governments are thrust back and conquered at the coming of Christ. But, because of Christ's advent, governments desperately seek to assert themselves and conquer God's people. It is their last gasp.

> The kingdom of God sets its throne on top of Satan's kingdom.

In Revelation, we see the subversive nature of the gospel. There is one true Lion King—every other ruler is a challenger. There is one true city—every other city is a false mirage. "To trace the outline of Christ's dawning reign on earth requires that one trace the false pretension too."[5] John traces the false pretension pointing to

---

[5] Oliver O'Donovan, *The Desire of the Nations: Rediscovering the Roots of Political Theology* (Cambridge: Cambridge University Press, 2008), 214.

Rome. But his finger goes beyond Rome and points to many other nation-states to follow. According to Revelation, all governments challenge the kingdom of God.

The Return of the King

The end of *The Lion King* mirrors the beginning. All the animals of the kingdom come to Pride Rock to see a renewal covenant. They saw Simba announced and now they see his kingdom advance. The posterity of the king will continue. The animals line up and watch as their conquering king announces his continual reign.

We actually do something similar. If you live in a city where a sports team has won a championship, you probably know what happens next—a downtown parade. People gather to welcome and celebrate the team and their accomplishments. They lavish praise on the athletes for the recognition they have brought to the city, and the athletes show their appreciation for the adoring fans.

This event is not novel. It is rooted deep in history. It was called a *parousia* (Greek) or *adventus* (Latin) in Greco-Roman times. These terms refer to the presence or coming of a person of high rank.

In New Testament times, these terms referred primarily to emperors and warlords visiting a province. *Adventus* was used for the arrival of a Caesar. Josephus, the Jewish historian, recorded the *parousia* of Vespasian to Rome and how its citizens came out to meet him.[6]

People would decorate the city and proceed to meet the returning figure outside the city walls. They would carry flowers, palm

---

[6] Josephus, *Jewish War*, 7.4.1.

branches, light, and incense. Singing and acclamation would flow from their lips as they accompanied the ruler into the city.

In the case of an emperor, he would meet with the local senate, and they would declare him the benefactor and savior of his subjects. When an emperor arrived, he could be welcomed as a god. Emperors were proclaimed as "always victorious" and "unconquered."

Sometimes coins were minted, and monuments erected to commemorate the beginning of a new era. This made the emperor's presence ubiquitous through imperial images. We even have evidence of an inscription on a coin that says *Adventus Augusti*.

Paul and other biblical authors pick up on this imagery and employ it to describe Jesus's second coming (1 Thess. 2:19; 3:13; 4:15; 5:23; 2 Thess. 2:1, 8–9). The apostle depicts Jesus's return in political terms—the return of an emperor.

Paul understood Jesus had proclaimed a political message, established political communities, and would have a political return. Therefore, when Paul endeavored to describe Jesus's return, he reached for the image of a conquering Caesar returning to his city.

The *Adventus Augusti* and *Adventus Christi* share common language, but they also oppose one another. The comparison invites contrast.

Paul links the coming of Caesar with the *adventus* of Satan (2 Thess. 2:9). Most suppose this reference is to Emperor Caligula. He set up his statue in the Holy of Holies in AD 40. But it also refers to rulers past and present. These figures exalt themselves above every idol and sit in the temple proclaiming their divinity (2 Thess. 2:4).

The point is Jesus's coming is strongly contrasted to Caesar's coming. He doesn't come from a distant land but from heaven. He is worthy to enter the temple because he descends from heaven as the King of the cosmos. He does so with a shout, the cry of an archangel, and the sound of a trumpet. These are war-cries! This battle is frightful news for those who spurn him and persecute his people (1 Thess. 4:13–18).

The coming of Jesus will be vengeful and full of fire on those who don't know God and don't obey the gospel (2 Thess. 1:8–10). Revelation says Jesus comes on a white horse to make war. He has many crowns, his robes are dipped in blood, and a sharp sword comes from his mouth. On his robe and thigh is written: King of kings and Lord of lords (Rev. 19:16).

Christ's *parousia* completes the redemption of the redeemed. It is their vindication and glorification. When Jesus descends, the dead in Christ rise first, and then those who are still alive on the earth meet Jesus in the air (1 Thess. 4:16–17). This is the victory parade for Jesus. All his people, both dead and alive, escort him into the city. It is on that day Jesus is glorified by his saints, giving relief to the suffering.

Paul explicitly contrasts the peace Rome promised to bring with the peace Christ would bring at his return. When those who oppose Christians claim, "Peace and security," judgment will come on them. This is a clear allusion to the *Pax Romana* (Roman peace). Paul says Christ will reverse it at his return. Christ's return will mean destruction for God's enemies (1 Thess. 5:1–3) but *Pax Christi* for Christ-followers (5:4–10).

The subversive nature of Christ's *parousia* couldn't be more apparent. Christians in Thessalonica were being persecuted, maybe because they too were defying Caesar's decrees. Christ's coming shows his kingdom would conquer all other kingdoms. Jesus came as true God of true God, while the others were only pretenders. Their work was sourced in Satan; Jesus's work was sourced in the Father. The *Adventus Augusti* and *Adventus Christi* could not coexist. The Lion will return and vanquish all other kingdoms.

Conclusion

In Revelation, there are two kings, two cities, and two returns. These are opposed to one another. Rome and Christianity could not coexist forever. Neither could Scar and Simba. A battle will ensue. In this way, Revelation and the Thessalonian epistles are subversive texts. Christianity is a new politic.

What are we to do in light of this political future? Should we seek only the city of God? Should we begin to establish this kingdom now? Should we separate from the kingdoms of the earth? Should we resist all earthly rulers?

In the next chapter, we will look to the political edicts which flow from our subversive future and the way of the Lion, pairing it with the way of the Lamb.

CHAPTER 8

The Way of the Lamb

Conquering by Martyrdom

Every generation faces a political choice.

Will we follow the cross in our political engagement or our own ideas? Will we let fear drive our decisions, or trust God? Will we submit to his way, or carve out our own paths? Jesus faced this same temptation.

In the wilderness, Jesus was tempted with competing views of what sort of politics would define his kingdom.[1] He was tempted to take up the way of *power*—to restore his nation by means of imperial authority. He could have all the kingdoms of the earth. But to do so, Jesus would have to bow down to Satan. Jesus knew

---

[1] I borrow the example of Jesus's temptations from Lee *Camp, Scandalous Witness: A Little Political Manifesto for Christians* (Grand Rapids: Eerdmans, 2020), 5–10. I have modified it for my own purposes.

his kingdom must come in God's timing and in God's way.[2] This was literally a Satanic temptation.

Similarly, we are tempted to trade our inheritance for an idol. We begin to think we can usher in the kingdom in our timing and way. This is the temptation of power, and Jesus would crucify worldly power on the cross.

Jesus was also tempted to *privatize his faith*. Satan enticed him to take and eat bread to serve himself. To satisfy his own desires rather than seeking the good of others. All he had to do was look at the stone and transform it into a piece of bread to satisfy his hunger.

Likewise, it is easy to become focused on our wants and needs. We forget we are placed here to serve, suffer for, and bless the world. Jesus knew if he served himself, he would not go to the cross.

Finally, Jesus was tempted to *spiritualize the kingdom*. He was told to go to the temple and throw himself down. His angels would rescue him, so that he wouldn't die. He saw the agony of the nails, whips, and mockery on the horizon. But Jesus could escape it all through supernatural deliverance. Yet, Jesus kept his eyes focused on the road to Jerusalem.

We too are tempted to try to escape. To view Christianity as not about temporal things but eternal things. In this mindset we hear things like, "Politics are unimportant" or "God's kingdom wins; who cares about the politics?"

---

[2] McKnight pointed out this idea of God's timing and way in McKnight, "Extra ecclesiam nullum regnum: The Politics of Jesus," in *Christian Political Witness*, ed. George Kalantzis and Gregory W. Lee (Downers Grove, IL: IVP Academic, 2014), 66–67.

Jesus knew there was another way: the way of the cross. His goal was fully political, but he wouldn't seize the mantle of power; it would be given to him. He wouldn't privatize his faith and let the world roll on; he would turn the world upside down. He wouldn't spiritualize the kingdom as if the suffering of humanity didn't matter; he would suffer, sympathizing with all the downtrodden.

The question is not *whether* we must fight "the Lion's war," but *how* we should do so.[3] Our political future shows us even though the King of heaven replaces the kings of the earth, even though the city of man and the city of God are at odds, even though the *advent* of Christ would mean the end of the city of man, the call is not to legislate this victory now.

The shape of the cross is our clarion call. On the cross, we meet the bloody and mangled Lamb. While John *hears* a Lion in Revelation, he *sees* a slain Lamb (Rev. 5:5–6). The Lamb is alive, but blood still colors his wool.

We are called to conquer. But the way we conquer shocks us. The slain Lamb becomes the paradigm of our conquest: martyrdom. It was the path Jesus chose for himself in the wilderness when Satan tempted him. The Lamb's army must trace the Lamb's footsteps.

> We are called to conquer. But the way we conquer shocks us.

---

[3] Mouw asks the same question. Richard J. Mouw, *Politics and the Biblical Drama* (Grand Rapids: Eerdmans, 1976), 116.

Conquer by Witness

Nike wasn't first called Nike. Initially the shoe company was called Blue Ribbon Sports. Bill Bowerman, the track and field coach at University of Oregon, and his former student, Phil Knight, founded the company. But soon they needed a new name.

When people inside the company first heard the name, they didn't think it would catch on. It was too hard to know how to pronounce it when one looked at it. But the name stuck, and is now one of the most well-known brands in the world.

The name Nike hails from the Greek goddess of victory and the Greek word for victory (*nikaw*). The name symbolized both the competitive nature of those who would wear Nike shoes and the success their company would eventually have.

Victory, in a similar way, is a big deal to every empire, and Rome was no outlier. The goddess Victoria, Nike's Latin counterpart, was their patron. Victoria was so central to Roman thought that she had a temple on the Palatine Hill, the center point of Rome's seven hills. She was regarded as the protector of the Empire.

Victoria was worshipped in the same way as any other Roman divinity: with prayers, vows, altars, and sacrificial animals. It was Victoria who was honored by triumphant generals returning from war. A victoriola—a carved statue of Victoria with her wings spread—was given to a triumphant sovereign and was a highly prized gift.

Even when Rome became Christianized, she still focused on victory. Constantine saw a vision of a cross in the sky. The inscription read, "By this conquer." But the question remains, how do the cross and conquering combine?

In light of the Lamb's victory, Revelation's main command to us is, be victorious (in Greek *nikaw*). This word in Greek means "to conquer, overcome, to prevail." It is no surprise, *nikaw* is a political term used in battle for conquest (cf. Exod. 17:11).

But this raises the question, what does it mean to be victorious in Revelation? By implication, what does it mean to be victorious today? Is it the victory of one nation over another? The installation of one supreme court justice over another? The passage of a certain law?

According to John, victory has already been obtained by the Lamb. We follow Christ in this victory not by raising a worldly army but by *witnessing to the reign of Christ*. In the words of renowned political theologians Rage Against the Machine, we "Testify."

We follow a politic of persuasion all the way down. The most revealing text for defining victory is in Revelation chapter 12:

> They [God's people] *conquered* him by the blood
> of the Lamb and by the word of their *testimony*; for
> they did not love their lives to the point of death.
> (v. 11, emphasis added)

John provides a wealth of political discipleship in this verse. He identifies the true enemy, the two pillars of the Christian's victory, and a statement of the motivation behind the conquest.

> God's people conquer him **(True Enemy)**
> *By the blood of the Lamb* **(Pillar 1)**
> *By the word of their testimony* **(Pillar 2)**
> Because they have not loved their lives **(Motivation)**

First, we conquer *him* by the blood of the Lamb. Who is the *"him"* John refers to in this verse? We conquer the *dragon*. The true enemy is not other humans. The enemy is not Rome. The enemy is not the opposite political party. The enemy is the dragon, Satan himself.

Second, we conquer by the blood of the Lamb. We conquer by being in Christ. We conquer by the victory of Christ on the cross. He conquers for us, but we enact his sacrificial politic. This leads to the third point.

Third, we conquer by the word of our testimony. We speak of Christ's victory. As this book has pointed out, too often we narrow the scope of this message, making it a private reality rather than a public one. But John was imprisoned because of the testimony of Jesus (1:9), and Christians were killed because of their testimony (6:11; 20:4).

> We conquer by speaking about Jesus. This is our main political witness.

We conquer by speaking about Jesus. This is our main political witness. Our conquering doesn't mean fighting, but pointing to and embodying Jesus's victory on the cross where he is declared King of the universe. This is how we stay faithful in a pagan society—we continue to speak of and enact Jesus's cross. This is the way of the Lamb.

Finally, John provides the motivation for how we can live this way. We conquer without violence because we know that to lose our lives is to save them. Like Jesus, our witnessing to another kingdom makes the empires furious, so they will kill us. But God's army submits to death. Our defeat is our victory. We overcome by loving Christ more than our earthly welfare. We witness even unto death. Death becomes our victory. Blood was the means to the Lamb's victory, and we must also become slain lambs.

The conquering-cross motif sounds like Paul in his letters. He compares his own life to a triumphal procession, but where he places himself in the procession is surprising. He is not being led in victory but led in chains to his death. He is amongst the conquered ones, destined for beheading at the Roman Capitol. However, through his death, he spreads life to the world. He has the stench of death, but that is his victory.

> But thanks be to God, who always leads us in Christ's triumphal procession and through us spreads the aroma of the knowledge of him in every place. For to God we are the fragrance of Christ among those who are being saved and among those who are perishing. To some we are an aroma of death leading to death, but to others, an aroma of life leading to life. Who is adequate for these things? (2 Cor. 2:14–16)

To be victorious in Revelation is not to attack the world. It is to stand firm under the attack *from* the world. It is to witness to the world, recognizing we all have a common enemy, but being confident that the victorious Christ has brought salvation to the world. The paradox is this: *for Christians, to conquer is to be conquered.*

Conquer, by Not Worshipping

The second way we conquer is by not worshipping. According to Revelation, the temptation is to worship earthly kingdoms. But we are to be victorious by not worshipping the dragon (Satan), beast (rulers), or Babylon (the city). The great enticement for us is to forget our true loyalty. Victory doesn't mean defeating the city of man. The Lamb will do that at the end. Victory means not giving the kings of the earth more than they deserve, even when they demand it.

Revelation is structured around worship. It begins in the throne room of God and the Lamb (Rev. 4–5). Worshippers gather around the throne and the multitudes fan out from there. They represent all of creation. This is contrasted with the temptation to worship other rulers.

When the beast rises out of the sea and receives a mortal wound but recovers, people worship the dragon saying, "Who is like the beast?" (13:4). The beast who rises out of the earth also exercises authority over the earth and makes the earth's inhabitants worship the first beast (13:12).

But if we worship the beast and receive a mark on our forehead, we will drink the wine of God's wrath (14:10–11). Those who worship demons and idols are killed with the plagues (9:20). Those who worship the beast have the bowl of wrath poured out on them (16:2; 19:20). John says, here is the call for endurance, a parallel term for conquering (14:12). The book returns to worship of God and the Lamb after Babylon falls (19:4). The ones who had not worshipped the beast or its image are given life to reign with Christ forever (20:4).

In every generation, we are tempted to give the loyalty due only to the city of God to the city of man. This is because earthly empires are characterized by requiring this allegiance. This temptation is illustrated in many stories from the first centuries of the church.

One of them concerns a woman named Perpetua from Carthage in North Africa (third century). She was taking classes in preparation for baptism when the emperor arrested her. Emperor Septimius Severus had determined to stamp out Christianity because he believed it undermined Roman patriotism. Perpetua was thrown into prison with other Christians to await a trial. Her father, who was not a Christian, came to the prison and pleaded with Perpetua to renounce her faith.

Perpetua refused. She was moved to a better part of the prison to allow her time to nurse her child. One of her dreams while in prison included a ladder. At the foot of the ladder lay a dragon. A fellow prisoner, Saturus, was the first to go up. Before he went, he turned back and said: "Perpetua, I am waiting for you. But take care; do not let the dragon bite you."

Perpetua said, "He will not harm me in the name of Christ Jesus."

Then the dragon slowly, as though afraid of Perpetua, stuck its head out from underneath the ladder. Using its head as her first step, she went up. When she reached the top of the ladder, she saw an immense garden and a Shepherd waiting for her.

The Shepherd said to her, "I am glad you have come, my child."

The meaning of the dream is clear. She is about to face the dragon, but she must conquer by refusing to bow to Caesar. By stepping on the dragon's head, she will enter the garden of life with the true Shepherd.

The day of the trial arrived. Perpetua was brought before the governor, Hilarianus. He examined Perpetua's friends first. The test was whether they would make a sacrifice to the emperor as a form of worship. They all refused, pledging they were Christians.

Hilarianus then turned to Perpetua, asking, "Are you a Christian?"

Perpetua replied, "Yes, I am."

Perpetua's father burst into the courtroom with Perpetua's son in his arms. He pleaded with her to have pity on her child. Hilarianus joined the imploring, hoping that the presence of her child would change her mind, but Perpetua refused to sacrifice to the emperor.

Hilarianus had heard enough. He condemned Perpetua and her friends to die in the arena. They were stripped naked, placed in nets, and brought out into the arena. Even the crowd was horrified when they saw there were women facing death. Their horror increased when they saw one was a woman fresh from childbirth.

Wild beasts and gladiators roamed the floor. A wild heifer charged the group and tossed Perpetua up into the air. Then a leopard charged. He bit Saturus, who was quickly drenched in blood. The mob roared.

Most of the Christians were already stained with blood, but the crowd began calling for their death. And so, the martyrs got up and went to the spot of execution on their own accord. They kissed one another as they faced their death. The others endured the sword in silence and without moving, especially Saturus, who was the first to die.

However, Perpetua was not blessed with a quick death. She screamed as the sword struck her bone. She bravely took the trembling hand of the young gladiator and guided it to her throat. Perpetua would now meet her Shepherd.

Perpetua's story is one of the many we have in the early church of those who conquered by not bowing to the state. Victory means not worshipping false rulers, even unto the point of death. The ladder that leads to the good shepherd has a dragon at the base, but we must conquer in the valley of the shadow of death. Our shepherd will lead us to quiet waters.

This story shows us we conquer by not worshipping the state. Every governmental system is animated by the dragon. They demand too much loyalty from Christians. Each party solicits this allegiance. They ask for our unwavering acceptance despite their evident corruption. They want us to be for everything they are for and against everything they are against. But we are *for* another kingdom.

We must stand firm and point them to their purpose and to the lamb who was slain.

We must conquer the dragon, not Rome. We are not against Rome as Rome, but Rome as influenced by the Satanic forces. It is the dragon who is after us. We must crush his head.

Conquer by Waiting

We conquer by witness, by not worshiping Babylon, and finally by waiting. But what does it mean to wait?

Sometimes in Christian circles this means playing the "Bingo" end-times prophecy game. We match current events with our conjectured apocalyptic clues from the Bible. We begin to check them off as passive observers.

One "Letter to an Editor" in the *Independent* said the following in August of 2020:

> Wake up America, Bible prophecy is being ful-filled before our eyes.
>
> Whether you like President Trump or not he has already fulfilled one of the last prophecies in the Bible prior to Jesus' return. Moving the U.S. Embassy in Israel back to Jerusalem and recogniz-ing Jerusalem as the capital of Israel is one of the prophecies that must be fulfilled. No other president in history has done this. But Donald Trump did.
>
> We haven't seen nothing yet. What the world is experiencing right now is just the tip of the iceberg.[4]

To be clear, this is *not* what the Bible means by waiting.

In the Bible, prophetic visions are intended to encourage responsibility and repentance in the present. We are not supposed to be sitting in a community center waiting to see what space on our bingo board God fills next. The New Testament doesn't tell readers to check off the boxes, flee to the mountains, separate from the world, or quit their jobs.

---

[4] Letter to the Editor, "Revelation Is Unfolding Right Before Us," *Independent*, March 21, 2022, https://www.marshallindependent.com/opinion/letters-to-the-editor/2020/08/revelation-is-unfolding-right-before-us/.

It tells us to wait. But this waiting is not inactive. It is a holy and hopeful waiting.

In Paul's letters about the end of history (1–2 Thess.), he argues waiting means holiness and hope. God's people need to become a distinct people in light of Christ's return. He applies this to three realms: sexuality, citizenship, and the church.

In terms of sexuality, Paul commands us to separate from sexual immorality, learn to control ourselves, and not harm others (4:1–8). Because Jesus has conquered, the church is to be a distinct people who steward their passions and protect the vulnerable. We are to respect that other people are made in the image of God, not using our gaze to exploit them for carnal reasons. Sex is a good gift, but it can be corrupted. The coming of Christ compels holiness, not political insurrection.

> Waiting means holiness and hope.

Paul also says this waiting will consist of being good citizens of their city. We are to live quietly, mind our own business, and work (1 Thess. 4:9–12). The temptation for us is to think we need to upset the order because Jesus is coming back. Lashing out at those who persecute us, meddling in other people's business, and quitting our jobs so we can concentrate on "spiritual things" are all ways Christians mistakenly wait for Jesus.

But Paul says heavenly citizens fly under the radar. He wants us to be "normal Joes and Janes" who go to work, come home to our family, serve the city, and love our neighbors. The loud and subversive reality of Jesus's return is paired with a quiet and submissive life.

Paul concludes by instructing Christians about the church. Rather than pushing away from God's people, we are to press into the community. Jesus's return should compel faithfulness to other Christians. He tells us to respect and honor our leaders (5:12–13). We are not to assert our independence because Jesus is our leader but honor those who instruct us. Then he tells us to recognize the different emotional states of the waiting saints. Some are struggling. Some are idle, fainthearted, weak. He says to be patient with them all and to help those who need an extra hand.

> Maybe the most politically vigorous action someone can take is to be a faithful citizen, employee, neighbor, and church member.

For Paul, conquering means waiting for Christ's return in holiness. Maybe the most politically vigorous action someone can take is to be a faithful citizen, employee, neighbor, and church member.

It is easy to begin to think only the activists do "political work." This is *precisely* what I'm trying to overturn. Since our whole lives are political, some of the most loyal citizens are those who do their work with all quietness and obedience. We can be political activists, but that is not the only way to be political.

We once had some neighbors who were not known for their political views. They were simply salt-of-the-earth people. They cared for those around them, adopted children who needed a home, brought treats to neighbors, were known as model employees, and were faithful servants at their church.

They didn't sell all their possessions and move overseas. They didn't march in protest. They didn't say radical things online to get a following. They didn't have a crusade they wanted people to support. They simply understood they were citizens of heaven who were called to wait for Jesus's return. In the meantime, they were to lead quiet lives, helping those who needed help and serving their neighbors.

Paul tells us we are to conquer by waiting. This does not look like end-times "Bingo" but sexual purity, loving one another, living a quiet life, honoring our leaders, helping the weak, and not repaying evil for evil. In many ways, we are to continue in normal everyday Christian responsibilities looking forward to Christ's return.

Conclusion

Our political future reveals our common enemies are the supernatural forces and sin itself, not Democrats or Republicans. The dark forces animate the division of humanity. Our call is to witness to kings of the earth about the sacrifice of the Lamb.

When Jesus was in the wilderness, Satan presented him with three options to escape Roman execution. But Jesus refused. He knew conquering came only on the cross. The way of the Lion must be paired with the way of the Lamb.

Our political future ensures God will vanquish the city of man and will establish the city of God. However, this means we must be more aware of the temptation of power, privatization, or spiritualization.

We don't eject from the politics of our nation or local provinces. We don't assume Jesus came to save people spiritually but doesn't care about their embodied well-being. None of these postures are supported by the Scriptures.

The New Testament says we are to have victory, but it defines victory in a surprising way. We long for a new home and recognize we are pilgrims on this earth, but we are not zealots. We are thankful for the land we live in, but we also recognize the government at times requires too much of us. We recognize Jesus came to install a kingdom, but it will be in his time and in his way.

Therefore, the next chapter will explore some different political postures we see from people in the Scriptures to learn how we can step forward in faithfulness. We must be politically as wise as serpents but as innocent as doves.

CHAPTER 9

Awaiting the King

The Way of Jeremiah

If you go to Rome, two iconic structures will lodge themselves in your mind.

First, the Coliseum. Pictures cannot capture its massive walls, impressive archways, and magnificent stonemasonry. The sheer size of the Coliseum dwarfs expectations. It is the largest ancient amphitheater ever built, seating 50,000 to 80,000 spectators.

Second is the Arch of Titus. The Arch is located on the Via Sacra, the main street of ancient Rome, leading from the top of the Capitoline Hill. The Arch stands fifty feet high, forty-four feet wide, and fifteen feet deep.

What many don't realize is both structures portray Roman victory over the Jewish people and their God. Titus's Arch commemorates the victory over Jews in AD 70. Etched in stone is a picture of Roman soldiers in a triumphal procession with sacred Jewish articles over their heads. One notable panel displays a captured menorah.

On the other side is a picture of a Roman triumph. An Imperial chariot contains both Titus (Roman emperor) and Victoria (the goddess of victory). Titus's arch memorializes Rome's victory.

The Coliseum is no different. The spoils of the Jewish War funded its construction. As is well documented, it was used for gladiatorial contests. Many Christians were punished for their disloyalty to Rome in this coliseum or one like it. It was in these spaces that Christians like Ignatius and Perpetua were thrown to the wild beasts. But a Shepherd awaited them.

What are we to do in light of our political future? These images might tempt the people of God to want revenge. The way of the Lion shows us Christ's kingdom wins, but the way of the Lamb shows us we conquer by witnessing—literally by martyrdom.

In this last chapter, I give four options from biblical characters from both the Old Testament and New Testament for how we can approach politics.[1] The first three are distorted views on politics, while the final one aligns with a biblical posture toward earthly rulers and empires.

The Way of Judas	Compromise
The Way of Jonah	Detach
The Way of Jeroboam	Utopianism
The Way of Jeremiah	Witness and Wisdom

---

[1] The idea for this way of framing things came from Jonathan Leeman (*How the Nations Rage*, 256), who used Judas and Jonah as figures. I added to and adapted his descriptions.

The Way of Judas: Compromise

Judas was a follower of Jesus. He sat in the best Bible studies in the world under the most learned teacher ever to walk this planet. He listened to every sermon from Jesus. He watched the love of Jesus overwhelm people. He saw Jesus walk on water. He distributed food as Jesus fed thousands of people. But when the time of testing came, Judas followed the way of power and money; he compromised.

Judas looked at Jesus's destination and saw destruction, not glory. Some even suppose "Iscariot" might be a Semitic translation of the Latin word *sicarius*, which was associated with the Zealots. If this is the case, Judas betrayed Jesus because he was disillusioned. He thought Jesus was coming to Jerusalem to conquer by the sword, and when he realized otherwise, he decided Jesus's politic was not good enough for him.

When Judas found out Jesus was going to offer his blood rather than shed their enemies' blood, he traded his heavenly legacy for a field of weeds. He sold out Jesus for thirty pieces of silver (around $200 today). He was nearsighted. He didn't recognize he would inherit a field of blood rather than streets of gold.

Like Judas, the temptation for us is to reject Jesus's politic of weakness, pursuing an earthly inheritance for ourselves and our children. We are tempted daily to trade our convictions for a little more money or acceptance from those seated in the halls of power. We compromise on our ethics or beliefs because it will get us in the right circles, make us the right friends, or pad the bank account.

For example, during the rise of the Nazi state, some German churches and pastors capitulated to the racist views of governing authorities. The state stipulated the dismissal and early retirement of civil servants who were of "non-Aryan" ancestry. What was the church to do?

In 1933, an Aryan paragraph was introduced in several regional churches. It stipulated the forced retirement of pastors who had a Jewish grandparent. The Prussian general synod, known as the "Brown Synod," passed the resolution, and many other regional churches copied this action.

The church in Germany compromised and accommodated to their culture. They sought the favor and protection of those in power. They attempted to shield themselves from persecution by capitulating to the kingdom of man, following the wide rather than the narrow way.

> We are tempted daily to trade our convictions for a little more money or acceptance from those seated in the halls of power.

We have to ask ourselves, Are there certain issues in our day that tempt us to capitulate? What do we not say because our culture won't accept us? What do we not do because we are afraid of losing power? What issues cause us to feel denial or avoidance?

It was not until June 1995 that the Southern Baptist Convention drafted an apology to African Americans for their complicity in personal and systemic racism. The convention acknowledged the role slavery played in its founding and its consistent failure to support civil rights.

The year 1995 . . . that was *150 years after* the denomination's founding.

That should make you stop dead cold.

Why did it take so long? And why are there still so few reforms at a larger structural level?

We too are tempted to compromise, to reject Jesus's weakness, and seek the favor of those in power. We must ask ourselves: Are we doing the same thing as Judas today? Are we blind to our actions because we don't have a historical vantage point?

Could we say many Christians vote for a certain candidate because of the allure of power, control, and favorable rulings? Or some vote a certain way because they think it will save the republic or win favor with the coastal elites?

The story of Judas shows we can't compromise. We must keep the long game in view. Those who capitulate to the economics of Babylon will suffer Judas's fate. Revelation says the merchants of the earth have grown wealthy from Babylon's excess and people have indulged in her sensuality, but they will moan and wail when she falls (Rev. 18:3–11). Those who compromise will have the destiny of Judas, the destiny of Babylon. Only those who follow Jesus to the cross will inherit the new Jerusalem.

The Way of Jonah: Detach

Because of the temptations to follow wealth and power, others respond with disengagement and detachment. There are too many enticements, too much corruption, and too much immorality. Like Jonah, rather than going to the city of Nineveh, we run. We take the first ship to another land. We decide the city is too far gone. We must escape the coming destruction—and we may even be glad the city is getting what it deserves.

As I mentioned at the beginning of this book, I lived for six years in Portland, Oregon. I befriended many pastors in the city. When I would return to the Pacific Northwest, some would lament the numbers of Christians planning to leave the city after 2020.

Some congregants would say the taxes are too high. Some would point to the riots, and the political landscape of the state. Others would point to the naked bicycle ride. They would say it was time to leave the city and go to a more conservative place because the culture was so far gone.

One of the pastors said he knew he couldn't legislate where people decide to live. A lot of factors should be considered, and this was an area of Christian freedom. However, from a discipleship standpoint, he was afraid people were running from a hard place. They were detaching and fleeing from the city of man, like Jonah.

One pastor said, "I'm not sure an extra $1,000 dollars on your property tax even registers on the 'suffering for Christ' scale. Why not stay in a post-Christian city and continue to witness to Christ despite the hardships you will face? We need strong Christians to stay."

Not everyone who leaves a city like Portland is doing so for the same reasons. But it does raise the question of motivation. Are we called to plant and proclaim in hard places, or to run? Are we called to find the parts of America where we fit in better, where the population votes more like we do, or are we to be a lamp set amid a dark city?

Revelation instructs us to be witnesses *in* the city. We are to warn of God's judgment and tell of God's grace. John speaks of two witnesses (the church) who will prophesy between Christ's resurrection and return (11:3). These witnesses are a light in the world, representing God's temple in the midst of a pagan society.

They will have authority. Fire will come from their mouths as they testify to God's political plan. But the beast will come and destroy them (11:7). Their dead bodies will lie in the street, and people will mock them. But after a time, the breath of God will enter them, and they will rise. They will be taken to heaven in a cloud while their enemies watch.

It is a strange story using metaphors to get its point across, but the meaning is clear. God's people are called to stay in the city of man, testifying to Christ, even unto death. They will suffer, but God will raise and vindicate them.

> God's people are called to stay in the city of man, testifying to Christ, even unto death.

What is clear is we can't disengage and run away like the prophet Jonah. We don't run and build Christian communes; we stay. We know our life is of no value in itself, so we remain to testify. The fire of heaven will come from our mouths. Ironically, the boats leaving the city might be the very ones that shipwreck our faith.

The Way of Jeroboam: Utopianism

The opposite of detaching is staying with the hope of building a kingdom without King Jesus. This is the way of Jeroboam. Jeroboam was the first king of the northern kingdom of Israel. After Solomon's reign, the kingdom was split into the north (Israel) and south (Judah). Jeroboam looked at the northern tribes and decided he would be better off without David's sons.

He would form his kingdom and separate from those who got in his way. Some even think his name means "his people are many" or "he increases the people." The people under Jeroboam said they didn't want any inheritance from David, the one to whom God had made promises.

> "What portion do we have in David?
> We have no inheritance in the son of Jesse.
> Israel, return to your tents;
> David, now look after your own house!"
> (1 Kings 12:16)

The north would form their own kingdom. They would look after their own house and build their own utopia.

In the same way, some of us think America can usher in the kingdom. You hear things like, "If we don't win this election, then we are all in big trouble. If we don't get this judge installed, America is in for it. If we don't get this law passed, there may be no more hope." So, we begin forming our utopian visions of society tied to the American dream.

This manifests itself in a "God and country" mindset. It is common with the right because they can be more explicit with their connection between God's blessings and Republican rule. At the extreme, governors, senators, and presidents from the right are viewed to bring God's blessings upon America: security, peace, fertility, freedom.

However, this is also true of the left. While they might not always give explicit religious language to their rule, the same ideology exists. The election of their candidate also brings stability, justice, equity, and freedom. The language of a specific God might be abstract, but the vision of a utopian society is not.

In secular politics we tend to slide into thinking in terms of exceptionalism, election, and messianism. Exceptionalism manifests itself in thinking our nation is God's chosen nation or gifted with a progressive ethic that we should spread to other countries. Thus, we are a chosen and messianic nation bringing salvation to the world.

We reinforce these ideologies with sacred rituals. In America, there are sacred symbols (American flag), days (Presidents Day, Memorial Day, Independence Day), hallowed spaces (monuments), cherished songs ("God Bless America"), and sacred texts (the Constitution).

Our political future found in Revelation and the Thessalonian epistles challenges these utopian mindsets. The New Jerusalem is not America, nor any other nation. It comes from heaven. Only God establishes it. The way of Jeroboam assumes we can form our kingdoms, separate from the messianic line, but every self-built kingdom is opposed to God's rule.

Babylon and the New Jerusalem cannot coexist. Babylon is not neutral; it is opposed to God and his people. They buck against his rule. They want their space to be sovereign. The two will ultimately clash. We have one hope, and while we can give glimpses of the kingdom here, we can't build the kingdom of heaven on earth.

The Way of Jeremiah: Witness and Wisdom

We can't compromise (like Judas), nor detach (like Jonah), nor seek a utopian future by building our kingdoms (like Jeroboam). According to Revelation, the way forward is *witness* and *wisdom*: the way of Jeremiah the prophet.

Jeremiah was appointed as prophet over nations and kingdoms (Jer. 1:10). He was a political prophet who spoke both to Israel and the world. Jeremiah held in tension several political approaches, recognizing each of them has a role to play.

The Way of Jeremiah: Witness and Wisdom		
Witness 1	Jeremiah warned his people against disloyalty.	Jeremiah 2:2–13
Witness 2	Jeremiah warned Babylon of judgment.	Jeremiah 25:9–10
Wisdom 1	Jeremiah told Israel to seek the good of Babylon.	Jeremiah 29:7
Wisdom 2	Jeremiah told Israel to hope in God's kingdom.	Jeremiah 25:11–12; 31:31–34

First, Jeremiah reminds us that *the political nature of our message doesn't merely mean witnessing to those in power. It is primarily a political message to God's people.*

Jeremiah speaks Yahweh's words to God's people, saying God remembers their loyalty when they were young, but now they have followed worthless idols. They have abandoned the fountain of living water and dug out their own cisterns, which will not satisfy (2:2, 5, 13).

In the same way, our political message should be directed primarily at our people. The focus of our message shouldn't be primarily critiquing governing authorities as a way of virtue-signaling. The meat of our message should press our people to stay loyal to King Jesus. We encourage them to remember their true King and their duties to him. That is our primary political message.

> Our political message should be directed primarily at our people.

Jeremiah says God's people need to repent, returning to the Lord and obeying his voice. He tells God's people they must turn from their evil ways. While it is popular in "political talk" to speak about the evils of the other party, the witness of the Scriptures reminds us we must first hold the mirror to our own communities. Before going to transform the world, we must ask if our own communities are transformed. Before presenting a political message, we must ask if we are enacting Jesus's political program.

In this way we desperately need a non-triumphal witness, a witness full of repentance.[2] John, the final prophet in the canon, follows in Jeremiah's wake. He is not primarily concerned about Rome but about how God's people can be faithful amid a hostile society. They must repent of their sins.

---

[2] For more on this theme, see Jennifer M. McBride, "Repentance as Political Witness," in *Christian Political Witness*, ed. George Kalantzis and Gregory W. Lee (Grand Rapids: IVP Academic, 2014), 179–95.

Rather than pointing to the finger at others, we must first ask where we have been co-opted by the forces of darkness. Then we lay these things on the sacrificial altar before God. Maybe then, the world will again listen to us.

Second, while the above is true, *Jeremiah was also not afraid to speak about judgment upon the state*. Prophesying to the church did not cancel out warnings to the nations for their evils. John does the same thing in Revelation. He warns those who would raise themselves up to challenge God's sovereignty.

Jeremiah says the Lord will not only punish Israel for their sins; he will punish Babylon as well.

> "I will completely destroy them and make them an
> example of horror and scorn, and ruins forever. I
> will eliminate the sound of joy and gladness from
> them—the voice of the groom and the bride, the
> sound of the millstones and the light of the lamp."
> (Jer. 25:9c–10)

Some will fixate on the first point and say we don't have anything to say to the city. But we must remember prophets spoke about the coming destruction of Babylon. Political prophets speak to the people of God *and* the state. The day will come when God will judge the nations for their sins, but that day is still coming, so there is time to repent.

There is a time and place to speak a word of warning and judgment against those who rule over us. But we must be careful to do so consistently, to both parties, showing that our allegiance is paid to a higher authority. We don't play the political games of the world.

Third, even though there was the warning of destruction for
Babylon, this did *not* mean Israel was to take up arms against
Babylon. To the surprise of God's people, it meant *Israel was to
pursue the city's well-being and pray to the Lord on its behalf.* For if the
city thrives, God's people will too (Jer. 29:7).

Exile didn't mean God's people were outside of God's will.
Exile didn't mean they were only to wait in separation from the
world for God's return. Exile didn't mean they were to destroy the
state. And most shocking of all, exile didn't mean they were to stay
and fight for their city. Faithfulness meant accepting God's judgment, and as they went into a foreign nation, they were to seek the
good of the city.

Since government is a common good, we should be the first in
line to seek the good of the city. This means being active citizens,
pressing toward and praying for the flourishing of our communities
and nation. While I have spoken strongly against nationalism in
this book, faithful citizenship is a Christian mandate.

We should be thankful for what the government provides and
even seek to contribute to the good of the city. We should be thankful for our freedom and many resources God has given us and seek
to preserve them and allow many more to partake in them. Politics
is about a shared life for the common good.

Fourth, Jeremiah also affirms *Israel's hope is not making Babylon
a peaceful place to live, but in God coming to rescue them* seventy
years later. Even though they are to seek the good of the city, the
land will become desolate. God will bring Israel to a new place
(Jer. 29:11–12). The ultimate hope of God's people is not in trans-
forming the city; it is in the arrival of God himself.

God will rebuild their home. They will plant their vineyards, and God will lead them back to their dwelling (31:5, 8). There will be rejoicing and hope (31:4, 13, 17). God will make a new covenant with his people where they will all know the Lord (31:31–34). Jeremiah's hope for God's people resides in God's rescue, not in converting the city, running away from the city, or in capitulating to Babylon's power.

As a political prophet, Jeremiah could hold all these things in tension. He was placed as God's prophet to witness to his own people and the nations. He called them to live with wisdom during exile, but to hope only in God's coming liberation.

Conclusion

I began this final section of the book comparing Romans 13 to Revelation 13. Can the two be reconciled, or do they forever stand in contradiction?

Paul says we must submit to the state, while John says the state is sourced in Satan.

John gives a picture of the totalitarian state—the state gone awry. Paul addresses the same state, but from a different angle. He claims states have a role in ordering society. The two ultimately cohere.

To put this most controversially: *the state can be **both** a servant of God and an instrument of the Devil at the very same time.* We need to carefully sift through what the state is calling us to do and obey up until the state demands something that conflicts with our highest loyalties (Dan. 3:12, 18; 6:10; Acts 4:19–20; 5:29). We don't do this because we are Americans, but because we are Christians. We are free under King Jesus.

Governments transgressing their bounds of authority is a tangible form of satanic power. Revelation tells us governments overstep their bounds when they begin to imitate God. They will require worship, demand loyalty, promise a new future, pose as a redemptive institution, and punish all those who do not comply. This is what was happening in John's day as the emperor required worship, and that day could come in any nation—even ours.

John's point is the great temptation for the state is to go past its bounded authority. As one would give a dog, God has given the state an electric fence it cannot cross. If it does, it will wreak havoc. But it will also ultimately be zapped. This judgment will come from God himself.

John didn't seek to reform Rome. He told it of the coming day of wrath. He instructed the church to be faithful during persecution. This was his primary political witness.

However, we must recognize that the Christians in John's day were a minority movement living under totalitarian leadership. We live in a different time and have laws that can shift things for the good of our neighbor. While it is not our primary task, we can and should be involved at a federal, state, and local level to work for the good of others.

We can protest totalitarian regimes. It might not be that they are wholly totalitarian, but rather corrupt in certain aspects. If the government's job is to promote justice (reward the good and punish evil), and if the government is doing the opposite, we should be the first to call the government to account for not fulfilling its duty.

We acknowledge the government's authority comes from God. That is why we can hold it accountable. Therefore, at a very practical level, the church should not be waiting for society to rise up in protest of the racial inequalities or sexual abuse our government allows. We should be leading these critiques.

Our critique of the state is not dependent upon cultural winds, but on the unchanging character of God. That means our prophetic voice isn't bound by what's popular, or what's *en vogue* on the left or right. We may speak on some matters in a way that will win us cultural brownie points, and on others in a way that will lose us cultural cache.

Our churches should be the loudest voice against racism, corrupt inequality, sex trafficking, pornography, abortion, broken homes, homelessness, child abandonment, and abuse, no matter what the culture is preaching at the time.

For too long, the church has followed cultural movements rather than leading them. Is this because we have lost the idea that our gospel is political? Is it because our communities have stopped reflecting anything transformative in these areas?

I suspect we have lost our prophetic voice on these issues in large part because we have capitulated. We can't decry segregation if our churches are segregated. We can't condemn divorce if our churches are filled with divorce. We can't work against pornography if our churches are filled with men and women supporting these businesses with their clicks.

It is time for political repentance. This might be our most powerful witness.

CONCLUSION

The City of Man and the City of God

Religion and politics.

According to conventional wisdom, these are the two subjects to steer away from at holiday meals. These two subjects divide families and friends. If you want a nice Thanksgiving or Christmas dinner, it's best to avoid them and talk about knitting, the Kansas City Chiefs, or the most recent Brad Pitt or Emma Stone movie.

Yet underneath this advice is the supposition that they are two *different* spheres to avoid. One is about our internal life, our personal beliefs, our heart posture toward the divine—the other concerns public life, the organization of society, economic theory, and community associations.

In one sense, this division is natural. In America, we have separation of church and state. They are two distinct spheres. However, in another sense, this division cannot be actualized. Most of history did not divide the two subjects. Politics and religion were not separate spheres but comfortable (or uncomfortable) bedfellows.

This book has been an argument that Christianity is fully political. It has a political past (gospel), a political present (church), and a political future (return of Jesus).

Despite the political nature of our message, we still struggle with political discipleship. We struggle with our public witness in a secular culture. This is because we live in profound paradox.

Understanding the Paradox

The paradox of our lives is that we submit *and* subvert. I have used these terms throughout the book and given examples and stories. Yet there still may be confusion. For maximum clarity, allow me to define what I mean.

To submit means *"to voluntarily yield to the authority of another."* Submission is a voluntary act that stems from the recognition that God has appointed governmental authorities. It is an act of agency by a free image-bearer made in the likeness of a sovereign God.

However, submission looks dissimilar for people in different situations. As one can see on the chart below, for those with power, submission means sacrifice and service. We sacrifice our own desires and power for the common good and obey governing authorities. For those without power, submission means yielding to the governance of those tasked by God with certain responsibilities.[1] Though the government will not always treat those with less power with all fairness, the response should still be to honor them in their work.

---

[1] Hannah Anderson was especially helpful to me in a personal correspondence and tracking submission/subversion along the axis of power. Much of the following she helped me clarify.

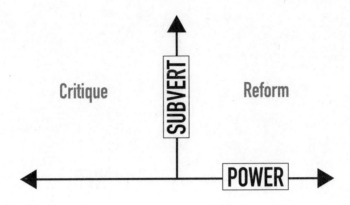

Subversion is not unlike to submission, though we are prone to pit these two against each other. It also stems from the belief that God is the one with ultimate authority, and we must obey him.

To subvert means, *"to use your words or actions to critique or undermine the usual way of doing something."* Subversion is the other side of obedience. We critique, challenge, or disobey authorities out of obedience to God. Subversion allows image-bearers to check or undercut those with power. Think of the biblical examples of Daniel, Esther, or the apostles.

Subversion, like submission, can be understood along two axes as can be seen in the chart below. Based on how much power or privilege one holds, subversion looks diverse. Those with more power may have opportunities to reform, while those with less will spend more time critiquing or protesting the existing norms.

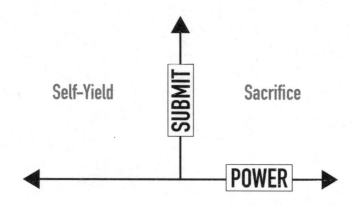

Both reform and critique has been addressed in this book, but in the New Testament, the Christian community did not have power in a worldly sense. Rome barely cared about Christians. They had no opportunity to transform the political situation both because of their social location and the form of government (consider the texts on slavery in the NT).

I have argued the early church's main approach to politics was to subvert unjust systems by existing *as* and advocating *for* the kingdom of God amid the kingdom of man.

They accepted and lived under a variety of institutional systems, for they preached about a city that was to come. Christianity is not beholden to one type of governmental system. It is malleable enough to live under a variety of systems. At the same time, their new way of life didn't only look for the city to come, but sought the good of all humanity and would have ripple effects in society.

Our situation is both the same as and different from the first Christians. It is the same in that *their* main task is *our* main task. We proclaim a new society brought about by the Spirit which is manifested in the church. God's main work of revolution happens here. Our political witness begins in the church.

But it is also different in that our political situation is dissimilar (in America). We don't live in a totalitarian state. In our modern society we can subvert by reforming systems and laws. There are good things that New Testament Christians didn't have the opportunity or power to do. That doesn't mean that we—who might have that opportunity—shouldn't do those things.

The Paradoxical Cross

The paradox of submission and subversion is showcased in the cross. Jesus is crucified on a Roman cross. It is his most calamitous defeat but also his most explosive victory.

These seem like contradictions. They are not. The tension doesn't exist because there are two kingdoms (as some propose) or because the Bible refutes itself (as others assert). It exists because we stand at a moment of transition, a chronological tension.[2] Christians stand between two ages. Political theology is so difficult because we live between the times.

> Political theology is so difficult because we live between the times.

[2] This line is adapted from Oscar Cullmann, *The State in the New Testament* (New York: Scribner, 1956), 87.

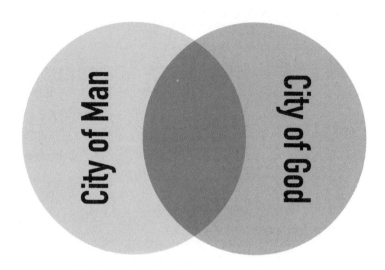

The old age is passing away, and the new age is both here and still to come. Conflict exists, but so does coexistence. Confrontation is inevitable, but in the meantime, concord is the call. The overlap guides us into the tension of our political lives.

The state can remain in God's present order because it possesses knowledge of good and evil through common grace. In this way, the state is good and part of God's creational purposes. Because of this, we can ascribe higher dignity to the state than a non-Christian. We know *why* the state can distinguish between good and evil.

We can therefore be under human governing authorities while at the same time being under God. One is paramount, but the two don't cancel each other out. Surprisingly, they meet. The old age continues to serve the church's mission. This why the church can ultimately pray for the kingdom to come, while presently praying for kings and all those in authority (1 Tim. 2:1–3).

But at the same time, the state has been confined to this passing age. It doesn't represent the arrival of the new age; it reeks of death and bears the scars of the fall. Because of this, we proclaim a new way. Like surfers, we ride on the wave of the future. That is the main method of our subversion.

But we can also be subversive in calling the state to their vocation from God. Knowing why the state can distinguish between good and evil gives the Christian the ability to subvert and critique it. In this sense Christians are the state's "watchmen" and must remain critical toward every state.[3]

Subversion coincides mysteriously with submission, like at the cross. Both are forms of obedience. We obey the one with ultimate authority: God himself. We submit because we have a higher politic, and we subvert for the same reason. Both must be part of our witness.

At the cross Jesus both subverted and submitted. As you can see on the chart below, Jesus willingly sacrificed himself because he held all power. Yet, as a lowly Jew, he also yielded himself to the governing authorities and to their God-given power. At the very same time it was his most subversive act. The greatest reformation movement began at the cross. His death was the key that changed the world. At the exact same time, the cross was the greatest critique of all tyrannical kingdoms past, present, and future.

A new King has arrived.

The cross is the center of our political theology.

[3] Cullmann, *The State in the New Testament*, 90.

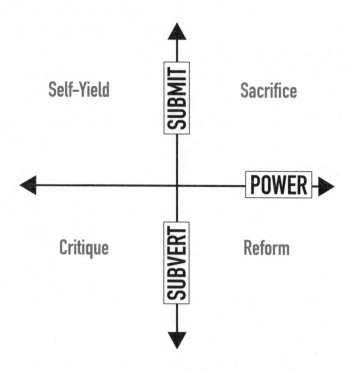

Self-Yield   **SUBMIT**   Sacrifice

POWER →

Critique   **SUBVERT**   Reform

Seductive Political Postures

Though this book hasn't been a complete treatment of political theology, I have focused on these two ostensibly contradictory realities: subversion and submission. One of the reasons we are politically malformed is our inability to merge these. We are discipled more by the talking heads on cable news. They urge either one or the other, depending on who is in power.

This has led to several political enticements I have identified throughout this book. We must ask whether we have succumbed to the following: a privatizing of our political faith or a partisan-izing of our political faith? To nationalism or nonconformity? To triumphalism or escapism? To utopianism or quietism? All of these temptations are different ways of describing the same reality.

Christians and Politics

Option 1	Faithfulness	Option 2
Private	Political	Partisan
Nonconformity	Citizenship	Nationalism
Escapism	Pilgrim	Triumphalism
Quietism	Proclamation	Utopianism

When Jesus arrived on the earth, he had the opportunity to join forces with several political groups that represented similar forms of what I have outlined above. He carved his own path and thereby taught us how to be politically active.

Jesus could have joined the Sadducees. They were the ruling class who assented to Roman rule in many ways. They capitulated to those in power so they could have a say in where things were going. This allowed them to "be in the room where it happens," and they justified it because they could represent the interests of Jews.

Jesus also could have joined the Pharisees. The Pharisees were the conservative group. They pursued purity so that the people of God might once again become the state. In this way, they renounced Roman rule because of its impurity. The state did not worship Yahweh or follow his laws, so they decided they needed to police Jews and help them follow the Torah.

Sadducees and Pharisees were toward the middle, but there were also fringe groups. Jesus could have joined the Essenes. Essenes were like Pharisees in that they prized following the law and purity, but they were separatists. While Pharisees rebuffed Roman rule, they did not separate from society. They thought it was best to stay put. Essenes, on the other hand, believed they could be pure only if light separated from darkness.

Jesus also could have joined the Zealots. They were the extreme wing of the anti-Roman resistance. They thought they could establish God's rule on earth with holy war and violence. They carried around daggers and caused mayhem for Rome's government by small but impactful chaotic actions. Jesus was crucified under the charge of being a Zealot.

Anti-Roman			_Pro-Roman_
Zealots	_Essenes_	_Pharisees_	_Sadducees_

The New Testament is a tour de force in critiquing all these systems. Jesus was not a Zealot, but he welcomed Zealots and discipled them into a new political community (Matt. 10:4). Jesus was not a Pharisee, but he spoke to Pharisees about the arrival of the kingdom of God (John 3). Jesus was not an Essene, but his forerunner John the Baptist was likely from this group, and he showed him the way of compassion and care (Mark 1). Jesus did not work for Rome, but he embraced tax collectors and proclaimed peace to them (Matt. 10:3).

Jesus was not anti-empire or pro-empire; he was alter-empire. He had both a tax collector and a Zealot around the fire with him at night. He recognized we are all political beings, pilgrims on this earth, patriots of our native land, and we exist to proclaim the coming reign of God.

His aims were entirely political, but political in a way that would surprise all.

Shrugging at Caesar

I said at the beginning of this book that we are not nearly political enough. However, in another sense, we are too political in the wrong way. We give too much power to earthly powers when we speak of them constantly. One of the ways to be truly political is to speak more of God's reign and thereby put Caesar's reign in its proper place.

That is what the New Testament authors did. If you count how many times the New Testament speaks explicitly of Caesar, it is quite rare. This clues us into a reality. By not speaking much of their power, the authors of the New Testament relegate their power.

Every day, first-century Jews were reminded of Rome's sovereignty as they passed coins back and forth in trade. They stood below statues and in cities filled with souvenirs of Caesar's power. They watched as people suffered under Roman governors' terrible miscarriage of justice.

In the shadow of Rome, their most subversive act was not to oppose Rome but deny its principal significance. Most of the time, they didn't direct people's attention to the shadow, but away from it—to a greater power at work.

The message of the New Testament is typically a declaration, not a negation. It does not fixate on Caesar's claim to be the "son of God," but proclaims that the true "Son of God" has arrived. Paul didn't say Caesar is *not* Lord, but Jesus *is* Lord.

Jesus didn't seek to unseat Caesar; he willingly went to a Roman cross. The Roman Empire was subsidiary to this story because it was simply a pawn in the hands of the powers of darkness.

Jesus was asked the most politically charged question of the day: whether Jews should be complicit to Rome by paying taxes to Caesar. He didn't respond by flying off the rail at their abuse of power. He also didn't speak in a soft and hushed voice, fearing their authority. Instead, he subverted their power—not by calling for a boycott, but by shrugging: "Give to Caesar what is Caesar's and to God what is God's."

We need to learn from this tactic. We are partially complicit in granting too much power to the current governmental systems by our feverish responses. By manically and incessantly speaking of them, we hand them the scepter. The media can't bear all the blame. With the rise of social media, "we the people" are the media. And if we give politicians 24-hour coverage, we endow them with influence.

The first business of the church, as Oliver O'Donovan has said, is to refuse to worship the powers that be. We refuse them worship by not feverishly responding to their actions.

> Not every wave of political enthusiasm deserves
> the attention of the church in its liturgy. . . . The
> worship that the principalities and powers seek to
> exact from mankind is a kind of feverish excite-
> ment. There are many times . . . when the most
> pointed political criticism imaginable is to talk
> about something else.[4]

The gospel is political, but it is political in a way no one expects. Portland barbers, South African lawn care workers, Chinese subway drivers, Missouri businesswomen, and Portuguese cab drivers all long for the true ruler.

Upon his shoulders the government will rest, and only he will bring lasting peace and justice.

This is our public witness.

---

[4] Matthew Lee Anderson, "Oliver O'Donovan on the American Political Environment," *Mere Orthodoxy*, October 30, 2010, https://mereorthodoxy com/oliver-odonovan-on-the-american-political-environment/.

Acknowledgments and Soundtrack

T hanks to Jaylenn Wong and Quinn Mosier for reading this with an editor's eye. Many others also provided helpful feedback. Todd Miles warned against the dangers of a third-wayism. Hannah Anderson provided both structural and conceptual questions that helped clarify points. For all future authors, Hannah is one of the sharpest readers around, so flood her in-box. (Sorry, Hannah.) Andrew Walker quickly noted this is more of a paradigm-setting book than a manual on political discipleship. Jonathan Leeman pressed me to be more precise in distinctions between the authority of the church and the state. He also questioned some of my more transformational language and distinguished the difference between what is primary for the Christian community and what is secondary. Taylor Combs believed in this project from the start and advocated for it. At the publishing level, he made this book happen.

The soundtrack for this book includes Taylor Leonhardt's album *Hold Still*, Caroline Cobb's *A King & His Kindness*, Rage Against the Machine's *The Battle Against Los Angeles*, Kacey Musgraves's *star-crossed*, Wilder Wood's self-titled album, Big Red

Machine's *How Long Do You Think It's Gonna Last?*, and Kayne West's *Donda*. I don't usually write books without James Blake and Bon Iver slipping into my playlists as well.

CHAPTERS FROM PATRICK
ARE AVAILABLE IN THE FOLLOWING:

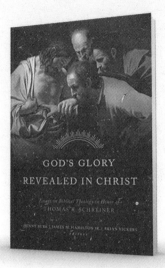

God's Glory Revealed in Christ
Essays on Biblical Theology
in Honor of Thomas R. Schreiner

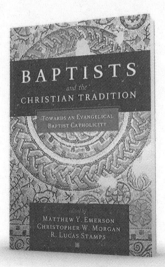

Baptists and the Christian Tradition
Toward an Evangelical Baptist Catholicity

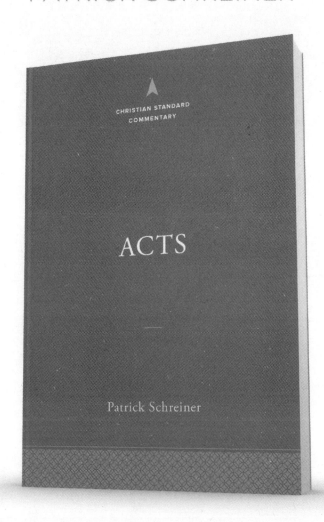